The Future *of* History

John Lukacs

■

Yale UNIVERSITY PRESS

NEW HAVEN & LONDON

Yale University Press books may be purchased in quantity for educational, business, or promotional use. For information, please e-mail sales.press@yale.edu (U.S. office) or sales@yaleup.co.uk (U.K. office).

Set in Galos Roman type by Keystone Typesetting, Inc., Orwigsburg, Pennsylvania. Printed in the United States of America by Sheridan Books, Ann Arbor, Michigan.

ISBN 978-0-300-16956-0 (cloth : alk. paper)
Library of Congress Control Number: 2010937665

A catalogue record for this book is available from the British Library.

This paper meets the requirements of ANSI/NISO Z39.48-1992 (Permanence of Paper).

10   9   8   7   6   5   4   3   2   1

To Willie

SPES FUTURAE

—

CONTENTS

I. Historianship

II. Problems for the Profession

III. The Appetite for History

IV. Re-Cognition of History as Literature

V. History and the Novel

VI. Future of the Profession

Contents

VII. Tradition, Inheritance, Imagination

THE FUTURE OF HISTORY

ONE

Historianship

The rise of historical consciousness ♦ The history of profession history ♦ History as a "social science" ♦ Historianship during the current crisis ♦ "Historical thinking has entered our very blood"

I.

Everything has its history, including history. (Everything has its history, including memory . . . but let *that* go, at least for the moment.) In most languages "history" has a double meaning. It is the past, but it is also the study of and the description of the past, storytelling of a particular kind. And what is the state and what are the prospects of storytelling — now, at the beginning of the twenty-first century? I shall — I must — say something about that big — very big — question later in this little book. But here I must start with the state and the prospects of *historianship:* more precisely, with the teaching and writing of history as a certifiable profession of certified professionals.

Professional historianship is more recent than most people think. Existence in history began with Adam and Eve, living in time and knowing that. After them, the telling and the writing of the past came to exist, but certain Greeks were perhaps the first conscious (and excellent) practitioners of "history" (the very word "history" comes from the Greek, where it meant something like "research"). Great Greek and Roman and other writers (including those of the New Testament) were inclined, some of them eagerly, to record and describe *real* events and real people, rather than legendary ones: but such designations as "historian" or "biographer" did not occur to them or to their readers. Many centuries later there was a whiff of professionalism in some men designated as "chroniclers," their appointed or selected task being the recording of certain events and of certain people. Still they differed not much from their Greek or Roman predecessors. Then— not during the Renaissance but, by and large, after it— came something else that I prefer to call the rise of a historical consciousness, particularly in Western Europe and England, involving changes in the minds and in the vocabulary of many people. Its marks were an increasing interest in history, even involving their self-knowledge. To describe this mutation in detail does not belong within this book, even though its author has devoted a large part of his teaching and writing to it, going so far as to claim that the emergence of a historical consciousness, say, in the seventeenth century, may have been as important as, or even more important than, the then emergence of the scientific method.

Still, let me illustrate this emergence but with a few words, examples in the English language. The *Oxford English Dictionary* marks the first appearance of history "as a formal record" in 1482; of "historian" about half a century later, at a time when the current meaning of "century" did not yet exist. Soon thereafter "primitive" comes to mean, for the first time, that some things and some people are still "behind" us; "progress," for the first time, means an advance in time (and not only in space); "century," "contemporary," "decade," "epoch," "Middle Ages" (for the first time around 1688, marking a definite age between "ancient" and "modern"), "evolution," "development," a little later. At the same time this new historical out-look arose together with a new kind of in-look. A clear example of the latter was the appearance of words involving *self:* "self-love," "self-esteem," "self-pity," "self-knowledge" first appear in English during the seventeenth century; "ego," "egoism" a little later — when, for example, "anachronism" appears, meaning something badly out of time: that is, historically wrong. (Consider that two centuries before that Titian and others painted biblical scenes and people in sixteenth-century clothes, with sixteenth-century Italian houses and villas in the background.)

In sum: the history of this development of a historical consciousness preceded (and transcends) the history of professional history. Of course, the former led to the latter; but my subject in this book is the latter. Some time around 1700, now about three hundred years ago, a few men began to recognize that a knowledge of history might be not only interesting but also practical — especially when it came to the relations of states. Around 1720 Cardinal Fleury, adviser to the king of France, wrote that "a man of mediocre status needs very little history; those who play some part in public affairs need a great deal more; and a Prince cannot have too much." The Regius Professorship of Modern History, established by King George I in Oxford in 1724, was restricted to training young diplomatists. The adjective "diplomatic" at that time referred to the careful study and examination of documents — in that respect a great French scholar, Jean Mabillon (*De re diplomatica*, 1681), studying mostly documents of the early church, and pointing out their errors, preceded the first establishment of a "scientific" study of history by a century. But something wider (and deeper) was going on. During the eighteenth century history began to burgeon and flourish as literature, especially in

France and England. There was now a great increase in the numbers of people who read for pleasure.* Voltaire recognized this. History is a form of literature that has the most readers everywhere, he wrote; consequently, he wrote historical biographies of Charles XII and of Louis XIV, for example. "History is the most popular species of writing," Gibbon put it, and went on to write it. Toward the end of the century Dr. Johnson, in one of his remarks to Boswell, lamented that there was not enough authentic history.

In more than one sense he was right. History as a branch of entertaining literature now existed. But consider that 300 years ago there were no such things as history courses. In the medieval grammar schools and universities, history was not a subject. There was no such thing as a history degree. People may have become more and more inter-ested in history; but there were, as yet, no professional his-torians. Then, about 230 years ago, this began to change.

2.

In 1776 or 1777 the first professional degree in history (more precisely: for the study of history) was offered in

* Two centuries before, Jean Bodin in *Methodus* (1560): "It is a practical impossibility for the man who writes to give pleasure, to impart the truth of the matter." Always?

the university of Göttingen in Germany. This had been promoted by August Ludwig von Schlözer, who insisted that history was more than storytelling, and more than the memorization of a past; that it was philosophy, too, connecting results with causes. During the next one hundred years this originally German model and practice and certification spread across the civilized world. On a map of Europe one could mark the advance of the history Ph.D. in the nineteenth century, from Spain to Russia. In the United States the first doctorate in history was established in Johns Hopkins University, Baltimore, in 1881.* We may therefore state this generalization:

During the eighteenth century history was regarded
    as a form of literature;
During the nineteenth century history was regarded
    as a science;
And often during the twentieth century, especially
    in the United States, as a "social science."†

* England was oddly — or not so oddly — an exception. There the first Ph.D. in history was not given until the early twentieth century in Cambridge. But the British college and university system and its degrees were different from the German (and other European) practices. Still, through the nineteenth century the civilization of the British Isles was enriched by the works of great historians in many fields.

† Before going further, a remark about the problems of the words "science" and "scientist" in the English language. The German word for science, *Wissenschaft*, is broader than the English word: among other differences, it also encompasses "knowledge," indeed, *serious* knowl-

So regarded — and so practiced. This, originally German, practice of training and certifying professional historians became near-universal. What were — and still are — its practical applications? Above all, there was — and still is — the idealized standard of objectivity. Or, in Germany, especially the insistence on "the scientific method," the proper application of which will (or ought to) result in the achievement of writing a portion of history "wie es eigentlich gewesen," "as it actually was" — the maxim of the great German historian Leopold von Ranke, whose life and work extended almost over the entire nineteenth century. He had his personal shortcomings, and he had his prejudices: but this was a noble ideal that should not be criticized in retrospect. He was not the first historian who was eager to find and then to extol the supreme worth of documents; but he was among the first to insist on a categorical difference between "primary" and "secondary" sources: the first having been written or spoken by the subject of research, the second an account of acts or words reported

---

edge. In English "scientist," that is, a practitioner of science, appears only in 1851. And in English, according to the *Oxford English Dictionary,* "science" almost exclusively means "natural and physical science" — a narrowing of an earlier sense (before 1903 "science" in Oxford was applicable even to philosophy, a usage that the *OED* now marks as obsolete). Thus, while the applications of the scientific method have spread, the sense and the meaning of "science" have narrowed — the opposite of the development of "history."

or recorded by someone else. Another German institution was that of the seminar, in most of which graduate students work under the guidance of their professor, studying documents and preparing their application. Yet another consequence: the professional dissertation — a more or less original work or monograph, a study of a single subject, no matter how limited, but based mostly on the student's discovery and application of primary sources, in full employment of the scientific method — finally qualifying him to be admitted to the guild of professional historians. This practice, and the "guild" idea, were taken from the medieval standards of the order of German guilds of craftsmen, where admittance to a guild required (a) training of the apprentice by a master craftsman, (b) the former's production of an original piece of work, whence the word "masterpiece."

The results of these standards and practices of nineteenth-century historical science were tremendous. So many of the great works written by nineteenth-century historians remain not only valuable but inspiring even now. There were, too, conditions that had made their achievements possible (though not necessarily easier). One was the gradual opening of archives, whence the accessibility of primary sources to more and more scholars. Another circumstance was that the "guilds" were still small. As late as, say, 1860, it was possible for a wide-reading historian who also knew two or more languages to be aware of almost all publications by other professional historians in his "field" and even beyond that. Moreover, the establishment and the remunerations of his professorship allowed him to pursue his research largely at his leisure. (Of these conditions the last still may exist, while the previous one no longer does.)

A classic representative of these then new conditions was the great English historian Lord Acton. He read and spoke at least six languages. There are evidences that in the 1860s, when the first scholarly historical periodical journals began, including articles, bibliographies, and lists of lately published books and document collections, Acton read an astonishing amount of these, whether their subjects were ancient, medieval, or modern. This at a time when British archival scholarship may still have lagged behind that in Germany and France. (Yet it was Acton who was instrumental in founding the *English Historical Review* in 1885. Though he never completed his plan for a monumental book (The History of Freedom), Acton wrote very much: his articles, reviews, and essays, and the enormous mass of notes for the eventual sake of that book, remain extant and valuable. Yet he, too, believed in the supreme value of the scientific method.

In his noteworthy introduction to *The Cambridge History of Modern Europe* (1897) he wrote that, thanks to the progress of historical science, it had become possible to write historical accounts of important events that would be definite and final. It is this assertion of a definitiveness that we no longer have, or should have. (As John Newman said already during his lifetime: Acton "seems to me to expect from History more than History can furnish.") Had Acton understood that The Last Word on a subject means something else than The Case Is Now Closed? That history, by its very nature, is "revisionist"? He had not. He died in 1902, an unhappy man. He belonged to the nineteenth century, a superb exemplar of historical research and writing then.

There were, however, not only philosophers (say, Schopenhauer or Nietzsche) but a few historians who during that very century expressed their convictions about the limitations of the "scientific method." In 1868 the German historian Johann Droysen put it beautifully: "History is humanity's knowledge about itself, its certainty about itself. It is not 'the light and the truth,' but a search thereof, a sermon thereupon, a consecration thereto. It is, like John the Baptist, 'not the light but sent to bear witness to that Light.'" Even earlier Jacob Burckhardt (perhaps the greatest of historians during the past two hundred years) told his students that history does not have a method. He told them one Italian phrase: *bisogna saper leggere* — You Must

Know How to Read. As true today, in our developing pictorial age, as it was true then. Perhaps even more.

3.

During the nineteenth century another predictable development came into being. This was the application of the scientific method to the study of large numbers of people. The emergence of the new science of sociology was but one outcome of that. A related outcome was the broadening interest of some professional historians attempting to go beyond the customary traditional subjects of the histories of states and politics and their leading persons. In a few remarkable instances, around and after 1910, particularly in France and Germany and also in England, this broadening also included deepening, a historical interest and study in the geographic and economic and material conditions of certain periods. In the United States, Henry Adams noted, as early as 1900, the existence of "the new science of dynamic sociology." Yet it was not Henry Adams but an entire slew of American professional historians who now believed in and propagated and taught the then very American and progressive idea that history was a social science. "What *is* 'social science'?" the fine American essayist and amateur historian Agnes Repplier asked a friend in 1912.

She had no answer to her skeptical query. Yet by that time many American historians had accepted the designation of their discipline as a social science.

Around the same time the teaching of history, its systematic inclusion in the requirements of high schools and colleges and universities, had spread across the United States. This was a largely bureaucratic achievement promoted by progressive and democratic historians who declared that the study and the teaching of history were eminently practical; that history should be "consistently subordinated" to the needs of the present. (James Harvey Robinson and Charles A. Beard in 1907.) Robinson in 1912: "Society is today engaged in a tremendous and unprecedented effort to better itself in manifold ways. History-mindedness . . . will promote rational progress as nothing else can do. The present has hitherto been the willing victim of the past; the time has now come when it should turn to the past and exploit it in the interest of advance."

This was American progressivism *par excellence:* democratic as well as progressive, populist as well as intellectual. Its main — and for a while leading — populist proponents came not from the East (Robinson was a professor at Columbia) but from the Midwest: mostly from the University of Wisconsin. Its main prophets were Frederick Jackson Turner, Vernon Parrington, Merle Curti. They were social scientists rather than historians, whether they would admit that or not. They were professional and intellectual spokesmen of a populist progressivism — which, instead of being very "modern," rested on the concept of Economic Man, not unlike nineteenth-century Marxism, though in an American version. Turner wrote that "today the questions that are uppermost, and that will become increasingly important, are not so much political . . . questions. The age of machinery, of the factory system, is also the age of socialistic inquiry." (This could have been written by a Soviet historian in the 1930s.) In his encyclopedic American intellectual history Parrington dismissed F. Scott Fitzgerald as insignificant. Beard wrote as late as the 1930s that "the expanded role of government would increase and not reduce 'the freedom of the individual.'" Etc., etc. Most of these historians considered and propagated history as nothing less than a social science — perhaps *the* principal science but a social science nonetheless.*

After 1950 the influences and the reputations of these Wisconsin progressives faded. After all, it was obvious that (unlike others, and unlike the French *Annales* school)

---

*A ridiculous example of this inclination was the methodical attempt at making history more scientific, produced by Sidney Hook, whom a committee of American historians had commissioned in 1942–46 for the purpose of establishing Historical Definitions. These were then published in a monstrosity entitled *Bulletin 54 of the Social Science Research Council*.

their broadening of historical inquiry did not lead to their deepening it: rather the contrary. Yet the notion that history was a social science lived on. Under that name the teaching of history was reduced in the curricula of high schools. The faddish interests in social history, quantification, multiculturalism, gender history, etc., were but new versions of the social-scientific approach. (Yes, an approach rather than a "method.") I must refer to some of these fads in the next chapter of this book; but here I must attempt to draw attention to something wider, which is the development of the historical profession through the past century, and especially in the past thirty or forty years.

4.

There was something American and illusory (illusory rather than naive?) in the propagation of regarding (and even classifying) history as a social science. But at the same time we must recognize that, as in so many other fields of life, the twentieth century was an American—perhaps *the* American—century, with a fair number of benefits. In 1900 there were few American professional historians who were regarded as leaders or paragons of their fields of study. But as the twentieth century went on, the reputations of many American historians rose to such heights. Much of this was due to the rapidly increasing contents and to the excellence of American libraries, many of them having become the best in the world. The quantity and the quality of their holdings began to surpass the accumulated riches of many European university libraries. Another contribution was the arrival in the United States of many scholars from Europe in the 1930s and 1940s. This transatlantic migration of books and papers and scholars quickly led to the extension of historical study and publication in many fields.

It was, and remains, remarkable that many of the admirable American teachers and writers of history (for example, Carlton Hayes, Garrett Mattingly, Charles Homer Haskins, James H. Breasted, Jacques Barzun — a random and necessarily incomplete list) chose to work in Egyptian, medieval, Renaissance, and modern European fields, rather than in the history of their own country and people. This was, and remains, a worldwide exception. It is natural for a historian to be principally interested in the history of his own nation — not only because of proximity but because interest, understanding, and knowledge, including historical interest, historical understanding, historical knowledge, are necessarily *participant*. Of course there were, and are, excellent American scholars of American history. The crisis of historical study and knowledge, to which most of this book is addressed, did not much affect their work. Their methods changed not much. We must not be critical of them for that. That the historical profession remained, by and large, unaffected by the cultural crisis of the twentieth century was a good, rather than a bad, thing. It is remarkable that while during the first half of the twentieth century radical and revolutionary changes took place in art, literature, physics, etc., by and large history (or, more precisely: its methods and standards, its teaching and writing) remained unaffected by that, at least until about 1960. Until then — and in many places even now — what went on in a classroom during a history course, or even in a graduate seminar, was not very different from what had been going on there fifty or even one hundred years before. That alone illustrates — more: it proves — some of the enduring values of nineteenth-century traditions and methods, so very rare in other fields of art and endeavor.

For many history still remained — and in so many places it still remains — a "science" of sorts. I do not believe that history *is* a science (surely not in the English sense of that word), but I will not argue that here — it may be enough to say that the legacy of the fine nineteenth-century historians must still command our respect, whether they thought of history as a science or not. So for a long time historical study, research, writing, teaching remained unaffected even during the cultural crisis of the short (1914 to 1989) twentieth century. But after about 1960 (an imprecise date, with many exceptions) this was no longer so. Many academic historians, in various countries, began to be affected by a, perhaps uneasy, sense that the study and the writing of history ought to be widened and deepened. At least some of them were now tempted by newer directions, by terms and methods customarily employed by other "sciences," such as analytic psychology, arithmetic statistics, etc., adopting them at the cost of relinquishing or at least compromising the former practices of their proud historical discipline by seriously considering what I, perhaps breezily, name fads. What makes a man change his mind, or at least the habits of his craft, is often a complicated thing. For some professional historians their search for new subjects, and for new materials of evidences, was probably genuine. For others this may have been inseparable from the desire to assert and prove that they — and history itself — must become, or be, more scientific as well as more timely. This is not the place — and perhaps there is no proper place — to analyze the purposes of serious men (and women). Purposes are almost always personal and only consequently professional. In any event, they responded, sometimes rightly, at other times wrongly, to what had become more or less obvious: a change in the texture of history and, consequently, in its subjects and in the very study and description of the latter. It has, at last, become necessary — nay, inevitable — to consider and research and deal with evidences and, no matter how fragmentary, records of the lives of great numbers of people in the near-present as well as in the more distant past. One, but only one, overall outcome of this kind of recognition was the rise of "social history," the study of classes or groups of entire societies. Valuable students and researchers and writers of social history existed in the past, emerging especially here and there in different countries in the first one-third of the twentieth century. But by the 1970s and thereafter all kinds of books and articles addressed to social history increased phenomenally, dominating the publications of the historical profession. That social history was something different from the definition of history as a social science, but also that much of social history amounted to not much more than to a kind of retrospective sociology, will be discussed in the next chapter. Here it may be sufficient to say again that these attempts to broaden and deepen the discipline of history were part and parcel of a sometimes honest yet also uneasy realization that the subjects and perhaps methods of old-fashioned professional history were not enough.

But this book, including this chapter, is not a tale of woe. It is now 2011, when the chaos of culture, indeed, of civilization goes on and on; literature and its study are in great and grave disarray: but still much excellent history is being written by professional historians. What has changed and

what is still changing are the conditions of their publications — and the circumstances of their writers. They are
solitary men and women — perhaps lonelier than they had
been before. Many of them are stationed in the oddest
places, surrounded by other professionals (often within
their own departments) who are uninterested in, and consequently ignorant of, their work. An, often unrecognized,
breakdown of communications has — inexcusably — come
about, in spite of Internet, Google, "blogs," etc. There are
innumerable evidences of this. Specialists in their "field"
may now find that other "specialists" in the field are ignorant of their published work. One overall cause of this is the
general diminution of the attention span. Another factor is
the bureaucratization of historianship. Consider that historianship is, and certainly should be, different from spe-
cialization. The nineteenth-century quip that a specialist is
someone who knows more and more about less and less no
longer applies. (Now there are intellectuals and professionals who know less and less about more and more.
Some of them specialize in "multiculturalism.") We ought
to pay more than routine respect to the genuine specialist
(whether professional or amateur) *because* of his authentic
dedication to his subject, which often amounts to more
than his desire for recognition. There are, alas, innumerable other instances when a person's desire for the status of
his historianship amounts to more than his very interest in

history. There is a difference between two aspirations: one authentic ("I am interested in history, I want to pursue this interest of mine"), the other bureaucratic ("I am interested in historianship. I want to be recognized as a professional historian"). These two aspirations may coexist within the same person: but we ought to recognize their differences. There is nothing *very* new in this. It was there in previous centuries. (Dr. Johnson described them immortally in *Rasselas:* the often cramped and airless conditions of competitiveness within a guild.) But there *are* more recent developments affecting professional historians. There is the still prevalent idea of professional history being a kind of science, with its certified professionals taking comfort in the belief that they are practitioners of methods and the possessors of arcane subjects of knowledge that are beyond and unachievable by common men and women. That such a belief is essentially undemocratic is obvious; that it is bureaucratic should be obvious too.

One result of the increased bureaucratization of the profession is the rewarding of mediocrity. This occurs now in many occupations, including the management of corporations and of institutions; but allow me to mention but one feature of this, involving professional historianship. Some time in the 1970s in the United States the administrations of colleges and universities relinquished the task of "hiring," of examining and appointing candidates, to particular departments. Now "search committees," composed of members of the departments themselves, were vested with this kind of responsibility. But they were often loath to give consideration to more or less independent minds who might rock the departmental boat. One long-range outcome of this was, alas, a perpetuation of mediocrity. Yet there were unexpected propitious results too: one of them being that some of the best historians found their places in provincial rather than in the grandest universities, to the benefit of such institutions, and of their students.

Meanwhile, the publications and the dissemination of new books in history have undergone substantial changes whose end is not yet. For about a century, say, from the last quarter of the nineteenth to the third quarter of the twentieth, it was not only possible, but professionally well-nigh required, that historians peruse the articles and especially the reviews and bibliographies in their professional periodicals (most of them quarterlies). But since about 1970 many articles and reviews and even the listings of new works have become deficient and/or inaccurate. Some of this has been due to the unmanageable mass of more and more publications; but much of it has been due, too, to conscious or not-so-conscious neglect. Before 1970 one could take it for granted that a new history book of at least some significance would be reviewed in the

American Historical Review or in the *Historische Zeitschrift* or in the *English Historical Review:* but this is no longer so. I know of cases when even the editors of quarterlies, etc., in specialized fields chose best to ignore and neglect the mention of new valuable publications.

All right — the recording of history was not, is not, and will never be perfect. But something else has now been going on. One example of this is that some of the best-written reviews of new books produced by professional historians are found not in their professional journals but on the large floppy pages of the *New York Review of Books,* to which many serious historians pay more attention than to their professional journals — while many of their younger colleagues would give their eyeteeth to see their books reviewed there, rather than in the professional quarterlies.

Much of this involves the now crumbling fence between professionals and amateurs writing history. Here note the word "writer." Amateur historians do not have the "ius docendi," the position and the certification and the right to teach in colleges and universities. But then the writer's instrument is words, and so is the historian's. Needless it is to point out that the greatest and finest history writers of the past were men who lived and wrote before (and sometimes after) the professionalization of history. What belongs here is the recognition that both the quantities and the qualities of works by amateurs (more precisely: of men and women without Ph.D. degrees in history) increased and are continuing to increase now, at the very time when the teaching of history has decreased in the schools. Again it is needless to illustrate this with names and titles of their books. It is enough to say that this development corresponds with other, wider and deeper, changes with which other chapters of this small book may attempt to deal: with the increased appetite for history; and with the growing, though seldom conscious, recognition that subjects of history belong to literature rather than to science. A new kind of literature: for it is more than possible that in the twenty-first century the best, the greatest writers of history may not be certified professionals but erudite and imaginative "amateurs."

However — and meanwhile — my professional colleagues need not unduly worry. There is, and will remain, a need, a very serious need, for professional historians. This is their particular task: the struggle against all kinds of falsifications, against many kinds of untruths, detecting and exposing them for the sake of us all; aware that the pursuit of truths involves, ever and ever, hacking your way through a jungle of untruths . . .

5.

There is — there will be — no such thing as a posthistoric man. "In short," I wrote more than thirty years ago, "we may be to some extent ahead of José Ortega y Gasset's *The Revolt of the Masses* when, around 1930, he proclaimed his angry impatience with the democratic mass-man who lives only for the present, whose mind is wholly unhistorical." More relevant for us is Johan Huizinga's statement, around the same time (1934): "Historical thinking," he then wrote, "has entered our very blood." Consider that this was a statement not by a facile optimist but by a patrician historian who, more than most of his contemporaries, was deeply worried about the decline of rhetoric and of judgment in our mass democratic age. Still, he wished to state the existence of an already embedded, and perhaps for some time ineradicable, condition of our thinking. Or: what the Spanish philosopher Julián Marías said (1972): "We cannot understand the meaning of what a man says unless we know *when* he said it and *when* he lived. Until quite recently, one could read a book or contemplate a painting without knowing the exact period during which it was brought into being. Many such works were held up as 'timeless' models beyond all chronological servitude. Today, however, all undated reality seems vague and invalid, having the insubstantial form of a ghost."

TWO

Problems for the Profession

From history of the few to history of the many ♦ Tocqueville about the future of history writing ♦ Public opinions and popular sentiments ♦ The sentiments of nations ♦ The structure of events ♦ After 1960, fads within the profession ♦ The prevalence of social history ♦ The present and future of history teaching ♦ Dangers of falsifications

I.

In 1694, the *Dictionary of the French Academy* defined history as "the narration of actions and matters worth remembering." (In 1935 the eighth edition said much of the same: "The accounts of acts, and events, of matters worth remembering.") Worth remembering? Is the historian the kind of savant whose training qualifies him to tell people what is worth remembering and what is not? To authenticate events and persons and matters as if they were fossil fish or scrapings of rock? Is there such a thing as a person and another such thing as a historical person?

Of course not. But understand—more: remember—that this definition of the French Academy, even though not necessarily composed by aristocratic Frenchmen, belonged to an aristocratic age which is now past. Then indeed some men and women mattered more than others —not in God's eyes but in people's eyes. They "made history"—though not always, and not wholly so, not even then. A century before the French Academy Shakespeare may have understood things better. In *Henry V* he wrote: "There is a history in all men's lives."

And so it is, and was, and ever will be. Every person is a historical person. Consequently: every source is a historical source. True enough. "Enough": but not *absolutely*. I have often thought that historians ought to reverse the logical—yes, logical—sequence of the words of the old Irish biddy who said of the gossip about the young widow up the street: "It is not true; but it is true enough." Historians ought to say (or at least think) about every "source," every document, every kind of evidence: "It *is* true; but perhaps not *quite* true enough." As Owen Chadwick, one of the finest living historians, wrote: "All historical events are in part mysterious." And "mysterious" does not at all mean "untruthful." As Kierkegaard put it: Absolute Truth belongs to God, not to us: what is given to us is the pursuit of truth.

Every historian worth his salt ought to know this. But

the pursuit of truth—its conditions, its circumstances, its very practices—do not remain the same. That pursuit changes through the ages. We are now in the midst of the democratic age, when we have to consider not only the conditions and circumstances of the material lives but the thinking and the beliefs of large numbers of people, in whose name history is now supposed to be "made." And this means a new and difficult set of problems for professional historians—because the very structures of powers, of politics, of society, of thinking have been changing. Perhaps even the structure of contemporary history, of its events—how and why (and when) this or that happened or happens.

2.

Tocqueville foresaw this. After he had come to America, he wrote his two volumes of *Democracy in America:* in its second volume he included a short chapter about how history will be written in the democratic age (a chapter seldom noticed or read by professional historians). He was not a historian when he wrote that chapter and book. His great and largely unprecedented achievement of a history of the Old Regime and the Revolution came later (not long before the end of his, alas, short life). Yet well before that we can easily recognize his historical vision, according to which even more important than the accepted division of history into Ancient and Medieval and Modern epochs the essential difference is that between something like aristocratic and something like democratic ages of history, from history "made" by the few to history "made" by the many. And the problem is less than the definition of "few" and "many": it is how it was, and still is, "made."

He was aware of this long before he chose to write his immortal histories of late eighteenth-century France. His *Democracy in America* was a proper and precise and honest title. His main interest was democracy, even more than the United States. In the 1830s the United States was (almost) a singular example, a representation, perhaps even a partial incarnation, of the then coming democratic epoch. But my subject is not Tocqueville, save for the purpose of illustration. It is the problem of history in a mass democratic age. Consequently a last remark — or perhaps a short excursus — about Tocqueville and America. At the time of his journey and of his writing the United States was — at least to a large extent — exceptional. Well, more than 180 years later it is — at least much of it — no longer so. Many years ago I wrote that the time may have come to compose a book that would be Tocqueville reversed, including his title: not "Democracy in America" but "American Democracy": how, and why, and in what ways does now American democracy differ from that of the rest of the world whose nations have embraced the principle of popular sovereignty; from, say, German or Finnish or Bulgarian or Japanese democracy? That could be the subject for a comparative political scientist. Important, for our purposes, is the recognition that *American* democracy is no longer categorically exceptional — even though most Americans profess and believe that they and their nation and government *are* exceptional.

That, however, is another story — though it relates to the subject of this chapter, which is that the most important matter of history may be what (and why, and how, and when) people think and believe — especially in the long run, which is something quite different from M. Braudel's *longue durée,* of which a brief mention will be made later in this chapter.

3.

So the subjects of history have changed — or they had to change. From the histories of states and of their governments to the histories of societies, indeed to the histories of peoples. And here we run against the first, the basic problem, which is: who are the people? It is not only that there are many of them, whence the quantities of information about them may be enormous (and/or inexact). The problem is the quality (and the authenticity) of these either fragmentary or unmanageable materials. Do the people speak, or act together? Sometimes, but not often. A statement made, or even a thought uttered, by Napoleon or Lincoln is one thing; it may be recorded. But a statement by "the people" is almost always a statement made in the name of the people, whence the problem of its authenticity. Here is the problem of democratic history: instead of being singular, authentic and down to earth, its evidences are often generalized and abstract, even when numerically recoverable for electoral or statistical purposes. A statement made in the name of a people *may* correspond to a choice of words or wishes made by the people themselves: but seldom exactly or definitively so.

"Choice" is the operative word: because people, as well as their individual components, do not "have" ideas; they choose them. When it comes to political elections, their choices are largely predetermined, ready-made for them, presented to them with few alternatives. At times the results of an election reflect the wishes and the choices of people, by and large; there are other times and circumstances when the results of an election do not really reflect their inclinations and hardly even reflect their beliefs. Many of the same questions prevail with public opinion polls.* That very term is often misleading. It is not only that the questions posed by the public opinion pollsters are predetermined and therefore limited. It is that Public Opinion was largely a nineteenth-century phenomenon. Yes, as Pascal wrote nearly 400 years ago, "Opinion is the Queen of the World" — but not necessarily "public." Public opinions, in the nineteenth century, were by and large the opinions chosen, accepted, held by the middle and upper classes — influential minorities then, but minorities none-theless. In the early twentieth century, when the research and the reporting of "public opinion" became a specialized business, its subjects (save for the prediction of electoral results, with their predetermined choices) have not been what is "public" but what is popular — and not so much "opinions" but sentiments. And to find and eventually re-cord what were and are (or to what were and were not) popular sentiments calls for such sensitive insights and such understandings of people of which not many, includ-

* Let us suppose that a lucky researcher finds an unusual statistic about popular sentiments in this or that German city or district at a certain time during the Hitler era. (There were such stabs at confidential sur-veys of opinion made by a branch of the SS during the war.) Suppose that such a statistical report is creditable, stating that in that place at that time only 20 percent of the population were convinced National Socialists. But: does that mean that the other 80 percent were actual (or even potential) opponents of the regime? Conversely; a statistic claiming that only 10 percent of these Germans were opponents of National Socialism does not mean that 90 percent were partisans of it.

ing professional historians, are capable. There are numberless examples of this.*

"Popular sentiment" suggests something less ascertainable or even graspable than Public Opinion. Its components are complicated; so are its developments, largely because of the existence of publicity. In the history of the United States we may state that the gradual transition from a constitutional republic to a more or less popular democracy ended in or around 1828. There was another transition, by and large completed around 1920, with the manufacture and the propagation and the managing of publicity governing the opinions and the sentiments of majorities. But here we are faced with another complication, concerning the, only superficially registrable, extent of a majority. The presence and the impact of publicity existed before, too, but a considerable extent of privacy still prevailed. (Consider here, beyond politics, the twentieth-century transformation of an "upper class" from Society to Celebrity: the former often private, the latter entirely public.) A majority: is it ascertainable? The existence of "hard" minorities and of "soft" majorities is consequent to determined and protracted campaigns of publicity: for it is possible for a numerically small minority to influence the extent and the ideas and the preferences and even the

* See one in Chapter 6, pages 154–156.

sentiments of majorities, a development not easily ascertainable by historians. (Or, in other words: the job of publicity is often to *simulate* the existence of a majority.)

Problems of quantity; problems of quality. They overlap, and they involve the very materials of the vast temple of history. Once we enter the history of the twentieth century and the history of the United States, we face a new problem of documents. The problem for a historian studying past centuries was, and remains, a relative scarcity of documents: too few of them, too few primary sources. But when it comes to the twentieth century there are too many of them, even of those in print. It is still possible for a researcher of a subject of an earlier century, including even the biography of a particular person of that past, to read, to "exhaust," most of the written and all of the printed material relating to his particular topic. For one researching history in the democratic age, topics in the twentieth century, this is no longer so. The opening of archives helps the historian, but not much. His problem is not only the unmanageable quantity of documents and "sources." It is their quality — whereby the essential distinction between "primary" and "secondary" sources has been losing its meaning. It is not only that presidents or other public figures seldom wrote their own speeches — but they had vetted them. During the twentieth century their letters or directives were often not read (and sometimes not even signed) by themselves. Now add to this the ever growing flood of telephone or teletype conversations, of e-mails and faxes and other "communications" unrecorded and untraceable. That condition alone ought to make us think — and revise — the still accepted maxim of the historical profession: is history the recorded past? No, that is no longer (and was it ever?) enough.

It is a remembered past — the reconstruction of which is necessarily incomplete and difficult, because a remembered past is both less and more than the reconstruction of a past from its remnants in records.

4.

The history of peoples is more complicated than the history of their governments, than the history of states. Yet states still exist, prime factors of history as they are. We may, more or less rightly, say that the Second World War was a worldwide struggle between Western democracy represented by the English-speaking countries and by Western European states and peoples; Communism represented then by the Russian Soviet Union; and National Socialism, primarily represented by the Third Reich of Germany. Represented, but incarnated too. Still, the states and the armies and the navies and the air forces of Britain and Russia and the United States eventually conquered

Germany and Japan and their allies or satellites. Surely during the Second World War, Stalin was the leader of a state even more than an ideologue; and so was Hitler.

Since the existence of states and their relations remain* principal factors of history, it is regrettable that the study and the teaching of diplomatic and military history have been recently diminished and even neglected. This devolution is rightly lamented by many of its historians and specialists. However — here, too, important structural mutations have occurred. Just as in political history democratization — that is, the inclusion of more and more people — has changed the structures of politics and of government, the framework of states, becoming filled by the mass of their nations, changed the nature of their relations during the past 100 or 150 years. Latest by 1914 entire nations rushed at each other. Popular national sentiments had become a main factor in the relations of states. Hence the proper study and writing of what used to be called diplomatic history has become international history, including more than the relations of governments, on a variety of levels and communications, and the images nations had and have of each other. This too was a gradual development during the

* But not forever. Consider the now weakening sovereignty and authority of states (and the popular respect for them). After all, the existence of the sovereign state was but one result of the so-called Modern or Bourgeois or European Age, beginning about five hundred years ago, an age that is now largely past.

past two hundred years at least.* By 1939 there were many examples when national sentiments, including the sympathy or antipathy that another nation evokes, became a factor in the relations of states — when in the minds of many people certain nations and states became not only ideological but cultural and civilizational prototypes.†
One hundred and sixty years ago Leopold von Ranke pronounced "das Primat der Aussenpolitik," the primacy of foreign policy in the destiny of states. He was right (and still remains so) — except that his concern was still with the relations of governments of states, and not with that of entire nations.

And here, because of the still powerful and principal

* A superbly researched early example of a historian's work exhausting the relationships of two nations on almost every possible level was René Rémond's *Les États-Unis devant l'opinion française 1815–1852,* in two volumes (Paris, 1962). Such studies about the relationships of entire nations in the twentieth century are still achievable: but because of the protean nature of their evidences they can no longer be exhaustive.

† I devoted a chapter to this ("The sentiments of nations") in my *The Last European War, 1939–1941,* mentioning, for example, the divisions between Germanophiles and Anglophiles or between Germanophobes and Anglophobes in many countries, and on a variety of occasions. In 1940 the main sentiment binding together the supporters of Marshal Pétain in France was not Fascism and not Germanophilia but Anglophobia. Another example: it is at least arguable that one reason why the so-called Cold War did not result in open (as distinct from clandestine) warfare between the United States and the Soviet Union was that their ideological anti-Communism notwithstanding, the American people were not particularly anti-Russian; nor were the Russian people particularly anti-American.

prevalence of nationalisms I cannot avoid an epistemological excursus. A human being has his relationships: with himself, with God, with other living beings, and with other human beings. But just as we can (and must) judge the character of a man best (and sometimes only) from his behavior with other human beings, the character of a nation, too, is often best revealed by its reactions to other nations — which amounts to something more than "foreign policy." What Marcel Proust jotted down in a note in 1915 is largely true: "The life of nations merely repeats, on a larger scale, the lives of their component cells; and he who is incapable of understanding the mystery, the reactions, the laws that determine the movements of the individual, can never hope to say anything worth listening to about the struggles of nations." (And yet: we must not draw biological identities between nations and individuals: we may attribute characteristics and tendencies but not "souls" to nations.)

Inclinations, tendencies are hardly separable from a person's or a nation's self-knowledge, including something of its history. A wanting self-knowledge, together with a wanting sense of history, is what separates populist nationalism from an old-fashioned patriotism. They may sometimes overlap: but patriotism is largely defensive, while populist nationalism is aggressive. (Or, as an old-fashioned British ambassador, Sir Horace Rumbold in 1932, put it in Berlin:

nationalism is patriotism illegitimately allied with an inferiority complex.) There are many examples suggesting and revealing that the more recent a national state is, the more immature and blatant its nationalism. An uneasiness of immature self-knowledge may be discernible in the characters of some individuals; it may also be there in the characters of some nations (at times even among the more mature ones, at least to some extent).

There are, alas, many evidences of how, in this very era of "the communications explosion," ignorance of history (including their own history) has affected decisions of national governments and of their elected representatives. Perhaps we should rephrase the famous maxim uttered by the Swede Axel Oxenstierna at the time of the Congress of Westphalia, nearly four hundred years ago: "Parva sapientia regnat mundus": how little wisdom rules the world. Too little wisdom then; but too much knowledge now, except that "wisdom" it is not. With all of the accumulation of international informations there is, alas, sufficient reason to rephrase the maxim: Multa stultitia regnat mundus — how much stupidity now hangs over the world.

5.

Peering into the future of history — or, rather, looking at recent history — historians of the democratic age may have to keep in mind that some time in the twentieth century the structure of events may have changed: perhaps not so much the "why" but the "how" and the "when" this or that happened. (Of course the "why" is ever so often already implicit in the "how.") Such changes involve the effects of publicity and of bureaucracies, probably remaining with us for some time yet. Here are two examples. How did the United States become engaged in the Vietnam War? Or: how did history become eliminated from the required courses in X University? (Notice the emphasis on process in the syntax: not how "was" but how did it "become.") Answers to such questions are, and will be, difficult to trace. In both of these examples the momentum of a bureaucracy produced the steps that after a while became irreversible. Note again: "produced." In the past bureaucracies responded to decisions made higher; they had not produced anything except their narrow applications of those decisions. This is happening now, too. But there is the other phenomenon, whereby a bureaucracy may be the originator of certain alternatives and of consequent decisions. It is no longer a ukase of a tsar that tells the bureaucracy what to do; it is the spokesmen of a bureaucracy who present the chief executive, whether of the United States or of a university, with a plan (often wrapped in verbiage) that the latter might accept. Now the historian's problem is that the bureaucracy, and its language, are often anonymous and impersonal. A first mention of a decision may be within the minutes of a National Security Task Force, or of a Curriculum Steering Committee of a Faculty. But who advanced such a decision, and when, and why? At times we may find a kind of clue — through confidential and personal informations issuing also from personal likes and dislikes, the latter seldom apparent from those minutes and memoranda. For here the anonymity and the hypocrisies of the bureaucratic process, disguised as they are by "democratic" procedures and trappings, go hand in hand.

"The tyranny of the majority" that Tocqueville foresaw did lead to popular dictatorships but not to a return to aristocratic rule. A saving grace: yes, history was, is, and will remain unpredictable — despite the mechanical bureaucratization of the world. In January 2000 Alan Greenspan, the then world-famous head of the Federal Reserve, pronounced: "Before this revolution in information availability, most twentieth-century business decision-making had been hampered by wide uncertainty. . . . Indeed, these developments emphasize the essence of Information Technology — the expansion of knowledge and its obverse, the reduction of uncertainty." Soon the very opposite happened.

Carlyle wrote once: "Narrative is *linear.* Action is *solid.*" (Cited by John Burrow in his magisterial and near-encyclopedic *History of Histories,* who then adds: "Narrative, therefore, though it strive against its own linear nature, must try, as it were, to move sideways as well as forwards.") What this means: include more things and people who are "worth remembering." That is, and remains, difficult. In chapter 20 of the second volume of *Democracy in America* Tocqueville summed up, in less than fifty sentences, his thoughts about "Some Characteristics of Historians in Democratic Times." As was his wont throughout this book, this amounted to a juxtaposition of what happened in aristocratic ages and what happens and will happen in the democratic one. Historians during the former may have exaggerated the decisive importance of certain individuals; those of the latter will tend to ascribe much of history to general causes. But then effects of these causes "are infinitely more various, more concealed, more complex, less powerful, and consequently less easy to trace." Historians of democratic ages will tend to determinism: "the principle of free-will is not made certain. . . . If this doctrine of necessity, which is so attractive to those who write history in democratic ages, passes from authors to their readers . . . and gets possession of the public mind . . . to their minds it is not enough to show that events have occurred: they wish to show that events could not have occurred otherwise." But they could have indeed. And therefore the very meaning of events that actually happened involves a consideration of what could have happened — a plausible and relevant potentiality.

6.

In this chapter, "Problems for the Profession," I now turn to something blatant. We have seen that the uneasy recognition that the subjects and the study of history must be broadened began to appear among historians around 1960. One of its outcomes was what I, perhaps pardonably, may call the appearance of successive fads.

Until about fifty years ago it seemed as if the writing and teaching of history remained largely unaffected by the devolution of language that had seeped into sociology, psychology, and political and also other "social" sciences.* Then, in 1958, William L. Langer, a prime diplomatic historian and a pillar of the Harvard faculty, declared in his presidential address to the American Historical Association, "The Next Assignment," that historians must henceforth advance to consider, study, and include psychoanalysis and its methods in their researches, teachings, and writings. His-

*Example: In 1950 articles in the *American Political Science Review* could be read by anyone without an acquaintance with a specialized jargon vocabulary or with mathematical symbols. By 1965 many of the articles could not. The first unreadable articles in historical journals, including *The American Historical Review,* began to appear after 1970.

torians lacked "the speculative audacity of the natural scientists," they tended to be "buried in their own conservatism." (Buried in their own conservatism? — weren't most American professional historians liberals and progressives?) Langer admonished his fellow historians "to the urgently needed deepening of our historical understanding through exploitation of the concepts and findings of modern psychology." (Langer was the brother of Walter Langer, a psychologist, who made — dubious — psychological evaluations of Hitler and other Nazi leaders during World War II.) Less than a dozen years later (about 1970) the very "concepts and findings" of Freudian psychology and psychoanalysis were beginning to be found impractical and insufficient by psychologists and psychiatrists themselves. More important for us: how was psychoanalysis to be applied to men and women dead and buried centuries ago? There were, alas, historians not immune to the psychohistory fad: but then a fad it was, and it began to disappear. Meanwhile, most historians continued to be interested in the characters of their individual subjects — that is, in the development, rather than in the "sources" of their motives and purposes. ("Character" was a term that Freud has inclined to avoid.)

The next fad, emerging about 1970, was quanto-history. Its appearance was probably foreseeable, one outcome of the realization that the subjects of historical study must be widened and deepened, including more and more people from the past, through the employment of scientific methods. Quanto-history, with its principal instrument: statistics. At times it seemed as if quanto-history (or "Cliometrics") *was* social history. There were a few graduate schools in the United States where mathematics and even calculus were now requisite courses for the training of professional historians. But the shortcomings of quanto-history were manifold and profound. There was (and is) not much statistical information anywhere in the world before the end of the eighteenth century. Of course "facts" and "data" could be (and, in some cases, reasonably and legitimately) tacked together from a variety of sources (parish registers being one such). But charts and figures were, and are, at best potential illustrations already existing in the historian's mind: props for his ideas (in such cases search, rather than re-search) and seldom its correctives. Besides, statistics too may be misleading (not necessarily because of shortcomings of their compilers). History is governed by the interests that human beings have in other human beings, in their qualities rather than their quantities. In short, soon after its celebrated emergence, quanto-history produced few readers — and, fortunately, few addicted historians.

But the inclination to recognize the need of broadening the subjects of historical research and teaching and writing went on. The emergence of the Third World and of "glob-alization" contributed to it. A result, latest around 1980, was "multiculturalism." Of course there were reasons for this. Both historical consciousness and the professionaliza-tion of history were European, and then American, phe-nomena. They were largely absent in the literature of even the oldest and most considerable non-Western cultures such as India, Japan, China, etc., because historical con-sciousness and professional history were something else than traditionalism. If — as late as 1900 — a Japanese or a Chinese wished to know precise matters about the history of his state and country in recent centuries, he had to read such narratives and accounts written by a European or American historian. But during the twentieth century his-torical consciousness began to spread, even though un-evenly, to nations and peoples previously unaffected by it. This was, and is, a salutary development. Yet — save for excellent specialists — the shortcoming of many American and European historians of "multiculturalism" was their comparative approach or "method." Most of them knew and understood some things about their recently chosen subjects: but seldom enough. For that neither broad-mindedness nor even genuine sympathy sufficed. One must write about people and things one knows best, which is the supreme desideratum of literature, including history. (There are advocates of multiculturalism who are ignorant of the very languages of the peoples they assume to study.)

The silliest of fads, emerging around 2000 (and, it seems, still running, though with signs of its weakening) is that of "counterfactual" history. Its very term is wrong, because history consists of more than "facts," and because its alternatives are not mechanical or geometrical. In mathematics X and Y are unchanging, fixed, categorical alternatives; they are also abstract. In human life and history they are not. "What if?" is not "counterfactual." "What if Napoleon had not lost the battle of Waterloo?" is worth a speculation, a question, perhaps even a short historical essay — whereas the word "counterfactual" may suggest that there was no battle of Waterloo. There is, and there should be, some allowance for historical speculation — because every human event involves a potentiality, together with its actuality. But — a most important condition — that potentiality must be *plausible*. "Plausible" means possible and not impossible. It invokes something not only potential but also actual, dependent as it is on our knowledge of certain people at a certain time. What if the German army had captured the British army crowded into Dunkirk at the end of May 1940? What if Hitler's troops had invaded England a month or so later? Such "what ifs" are worth thinking about, or at least keeping in mind, because they were evident possibilities. Their very *potentiality* made Churchill's *actual* decision to fight on so important. In other words: the very meaning of what happened is not separable from what could have happened. And that potentiality must be plausible enough to think or say or write about — in history as it is in a novel. That Lee won at Gettysburg because the Argentinian army had arrived to fight on the side of the South in 1863; that Hitler lost the battle of France because the Chinese attacked him in the rear in 1940 — or that at the end of *Pride and Prejudice* Elizabeth Bennet eloped with an Egyptian astrologer in 1815 — may be "counterfactual" but unworthy of speculation because so implausible as to be useless.

But now to a fortunate conclusion. What if the great majority of professional historians had succumbed to these fads? Well, they didn't. Much good history, its research and study and writing, still goes on nowadays, 2011. How long? *That* I cannot tell.

7.

What is still going on is the now predominant practice of researching, teaching, and writing social history. A branch of history, but not a social science. Social science and social history: we must distinguish them. Social history is not necessarily "scientific": its purpose is (or at least it should be) description, not definition. The concept of social science is both progressive and utilitarian: it suggests the subordination of history to it; its purpose is knowledge to be employed for the sake of the betterment of a nation or indeed of much of the world. A century after its predominance in the United States the appeal of social science has now faded — but at a time when the pursuit of social history is romping ahead.

Its purpose is the furthering of our comprehension of portions of the past. A respectable purpose — except that its practice and methods are, alas, more than often compromised by its purveyors. Here is not the place to list, or even give a few extreme examples of, what during the past forty years appeared as "social" or "gender" histories. In many instances their very titles must strike us for being ridiculous.* Some of them have made contributions to our existing knowledge of this or that people at a given past. But there is one general shortcoming in many of them. This is that the essence of most, if not all, social histories is economic — that is, materialist history. Yes: historians must consider and research the geographic and economic and financial and material and even biological conditions when they analyze and then attempt to de-

---

* See Chapter 4, 86–87. Also: "Cliometrics," an unattractive fad word (like quanto-history) about forty years ago (now just about disappeared): Bruce Catton in an essay-review of Fogel and Engerman, *Time on the Cross: The Economies of American Negro Slavery:* "A great breakthrough in history cliometrics is not, but it *is* a breakthrough in the field of publicity."

scribe a particular people in a particular place at a particular time in the past. But they must, even more, consider the unavoidable limitations of their research: that their sources for that kind of information are necessarily quite fragmentary and therefore limited, whereby so are their generalizations and projections resting on them.

Are material "factors" *always* the most decisive ones in the histories of a people? Contrary to the Marxist and also to the capitalist-determinist conception of history, what people think (and believe), and what they thought (and believed), is not the superstructure of their lives and histories but a, or indeed the, most important of factors — wherefore the economic conditions of their lives are the consequences: they *are* the "superstructures." This hierarchy of relative importances is not constant. The influences of mind on matter (and also their reverse) have changed through the ages. Oddly — or perhaps not so oddly — the influence of mind on matter, including the increasing spiritualization, indeed, the abstraction, of matter is (or should be) evident now, in the mass democratic age, in spite of the general acceptance of a materialist determinism.*

* This is not mere speculative theorizing. I applied this relative hierarchy of historical forces or factors to the structure of many of my books. There I attempted to describe or sum up the material or economic conditions of a given people at a given time, and thereafter moved ahead to their social and then political and then international circumstances and

Structures of relative importances; structures of events — and within the latter the intrusion of the mental element. We can measure and ascertain when and what pressure on a piece of matter will break it. (Or at what temperature a liquid will boil.) But when it comes to human beings "intolerable" is what and when they think they cannot or should not tolerate. The recognition and realization and the development of that is not a simple matter. What happens is inseparable from what people think happens. Inseparable: but not identical. Eventually people may (or may not) recognize that what they thought had happened was not really what happened. (And the promotion of such recognitions is one of the most commendable tasks of professional historians.)

People do not change their minds fast. The momentum of accepted opinions and sentiments can be constrained, slow, lasting for a long time. But that "long time" is not the "longue durée" that Fernand Braudel proposed in his grand two-volume history of the Mediterranean world in the second half of the sixteenth century. He deserves credit for his magisterial *The Mediterranean and the Mediterranean World in the Age of Philip II*. Much, if not most, of it

---

then to tendencies of their thoughts and beliefs, in successive chapters, in an ascending sequence of their relative significance. (Yet even the most positive and respectful critics and commentators of my various books have not noticed this hierarchical organization.)

is geographic, economic, financial, material history. It is an attempt at something new, defined as a *total history*. And yet: among Braudel's enormous accumulation and management of data and evidences there is not much — something but not much — about what and how those very various peoples along and behind the shores of the Mediterranean were thinking and believing then.* His portrait of Philip II, of the limits of his mind, reflects Braudel's capacity of human and historical understanding. But then throughout his book he suggests that Philip II did not much matter. And here we arrive at my main point: what Braudel means by "structures" and "conjunctures" and "the long run" is not what I mean. Just as the death of Philip II in September 1598 was not a great event in the history of the Mediterranean according to Braudel, there is "good reason for us to reflect once more on the distance separating biographical history from the history of structures, and, even more, from the history of geo-

* In this respect Johan Huizinga's *The Waning of the Middle Ages* (1920) may be seen as more of a pathbreaking work: for Huizinga's main theme and subject was *how* people were thinking and seeing, how they were employing some of their minds at a given place and time. Or consider Eamon Duffy's *The Voices of Morebath* (2001), dealing with the revolution and counterrevolution of religion, parishes, churches, and people in England (in the same century as Braudel's *Mediterranean*). Were the economic and financial changes, great as they were made by Henry VIII and his minions, more decisive than what was happening to loyalties, religion, churches, sentiments? Were the great changes in sixteenth-century England mere "conjunctures"?

graphical areas." Yes, this is so. But, says Braudel: "I am by temperament a 'structuralist', little tempted by the event, or even by the short-term conjuncture which is after all merely regrouping of events in the same area." No: it can be more (or less) than that.

"All efforts against the prevailing tide of history — which is not always obvious — are doomed to failure. . . . When I think of the individual, I am always inclined to see him imprisoned within a destiny in which he himself has little hand. . . . In historical analysis as I see it, rightly or wrongly, the long run always wins in the end." Yes: continuity is often as important, even more important, than change. But change is something else than "conjuncture." After all, "structures" — like landscapes — are, surely at least partially, man-made. And how? and why? and when? That is why social history must be not only different but more than retrospective sociology — which, alas, it often is.

8.

A book with the title *The Future of History,* written and published eleven years into the twenty-first century, must be suffused throughout with the question, laden with anxiety: what will happen to books of history and to the practice of their reading? But in this chapter ("Problems for the Profession") I must turn — briefly — to another, though allied, question: what happens, what will happen, to the practice of teaching? Of history, that is. Like the spoken and written word, teaching and writing are not quite the same; but they *are* inextricably bound to each other. Especially so because of the traditional conditions of professional historianship, since a doctorate or another high degree has been a prerequisite, enabling its possessor to enter a college or university department of history to teach. There were, and are, ample examples of respected professors preferring to teach not much, or perhaps hardly at all; of others, in the beginning of their professional careers, to have to publish and not perish; and of reputations achieved by others because of their published writings rather than by the qualities of their teaching. But here a few thoughts about the latter — especially in the United States, where the influences of classroom teaching have been, by and large, more direct than in most European universities. And here the practice of classroom teaching — that is, the lectures of a professor and the presence of their recipients — have not much changed during the past one hundred (or even more) years.

I am speaking of colleges and universities. (The diminution and the evolution of history courses in the high and middle schools is another story.) The essence of my argument is that the wish to learn more of history, including the inclinations of a few students to seek — perhaps — a professional career in historianship, has been almost always an outcome of hearing the lectures of a professor in a classroom and of his consequent leading those students to the reading of certain books. (In most universities in Europe professors' lectures [and often even the presence of students] matter less than the students' performances at the subsequent examinations.) I am not referring here to graduate practices, including seminars, but to the ineffable and unmeasurable influence that the teaching (and often the personal character) of a college teacher has had and may still have on his captive audience — or, more precisely, on those who are listening to him.

Will this practice of classroom teaching survive? Let us hope so — even though there are many recent developments compromising, nay, undermining it. One, perhaps the most insidious, development is the general decrease of the attention span: an almost universal phenomenon, but especially harmful for younger people. Its consequences are obvious and manifold. There is the fast-shrinking habit of reading among students, their ever more limited acquaintance with books. Books are now available easily, not only in libraries but in many places and forms: but the requirements of readings have been diminishing in colleges and universities. (The English tutorial system [or lack of a system], requiring a considerable amount of reading, has already begun to fade.) And the penetration of a pictorial rather than verbal "culture" — indeed, imagination itself — has now invaded traditional classrooms too, with many a professor showing a movie or directing his students to a film. And meanwhile many of the very topics of professors' lectures have changed, too. Will social or "gender" history nourish the intellectual appetite of a putative student in the way political or military history inspired students in the past? Or: will lectures broadcast through long impersonal distances, through television or other recording and transmitting devices, replace classroom teaching more and more? The unavoidable — sometimes nearly mysterious but in any case unmeasurable (and certainly reciprocal) — classroom relationship of teachers with students may decline and even disappear.

But that, too, is unpredictable, for all kinds of reasons. The captivity of willing and unwilling, of listening and not listening students in classrooms may still exist for some time yet. "The future of history," as indeed "the future" of anything, is a cavalier phrase. Whatever we know, or think we know, of the future is hardly anything but the projection (and often an exaggeration) of some things we see occurring at the present. Such projections are often wrong because of the unpredictability of history, its progress being neither geometric nor linear. Perhaps the best that may be expected from a judicious historian (or indeed from any intelligent—and history-minded—observer of the present) is his foretelling not of what is going to happen but what is *not* likely to happen.

This brings me to a, necessarily very inadequate, stab at the present and potential impact of electronic technology, less on the teaching than on the research and writing of history. Here I am more constrained than are others, because of my own lack of experience and knowledge of electronic machinery. For one thing, a by and large welcome change began to affect the techniques of historical research after about 1960. Microfilms and photocopying machines made access to the homebound reading of documents faster and easier. I too have benefited from these facilities of research for several books of mine (in my case I can even pinpoint my first such profitable experience: 1970). Further than that I did not much go. Yet what has already happened is important. The computer and the Internet (and e-mail) have made contacts and communications between scholars easier. The electronic retrieval of data and documents has made the search for such (though not for all of them) easier. But like every present and possible technical invention, these new facilities present new problems. It is not easy to determine whether the "research" in a term paper confected by a student, or indeed within an entire article or book by a certified scholar, is authentic. Another problem, not negligible, is that the "information" available on Google or Wikipedia may be (and often is) inaccurate: a problem compounded by the tendency of its viewers to believe that, whatever shown on a computer is necessarily precise and/or complete. (Note that the popular and accepted term for Google, etc., is "search engine" — whereas the essence of historical inquiry is *re-search,* as perhaps first exemplified by Thucydides, who wrote his history of the Peloponnesian wars, as he said, to correct and eliminate legends, false beliefs, mistakes.)

There is — yet — no evidence that these technical innovations have made the writing of history, the work of a serious historian, better. Neither is there evidence — indeed, some signs point to the contrary — that they have brought professional historians closer together: in other words, more acquainted with one another. What we *can* tell is that technology has made pictorial presentations of this or that history more and more possible. But here too problems exist. Pictorial presentations of scenes or episodes or persons may give the impression of something direct, three-dimensional, accurate, real: but in reality their production is very complicated, resulting in images and people seeming "true" but often not true enough. The pictorial presentation or representation of historical episodes can be stunning: but then they were chosen and put together because of their impact, on how they will look and seem — which is something different from the purposes of an honest teacher or writer of history. And even when the authenticity or the truthfulness of a moving picture may be questionable, the actual analysis of a picture or of a detail may be so difficult as to be hardly worthwhile — unlike the pointing out of a falsification in a printed book or article or indeed in anything having been written.

9.

The problem of falsifications is now greater than before, because of technology. Forgeries of historical documents (almost always for political purposes) have always existed. But new developments confront historians now. One is the technical perfection of the very materials of forged or falsified documents, the components of their paper, of their ink, of the typewriter fonts, etc. The other, more insidious, practice is the presentation of a scholarly apparatus, listing or citing microfilm numbers or other archival "sources" that are not easily ascertainable — or, even if so, require careful reading by a professional historian to eventually reveal that they do not prove the "fact" or statement they are supposed to confirm. I have confronted such instances of documentary falsifications or forgeries, especially in subjects relating to the Second World War. This is not the place to detail or even list them, except to say that they are often very cleverly done, by very knowledgeable people. (In many cases their hidden purpose has been a rehabilitation of Hitler. "Hidden," since in most cases their aim is to blacken the reputation of his opponents by the production of forged or falsified "documents" or "sources.") We cannot expect the reading public to ascertain such carefully done falsifications. But that remains the duty of professional historians: a task never ending, and never complete.

THREE

The Appetite for History

A new phenomenon. Its various evidences ♦ At the same time the reduced teaching of history ♦ Possible sources of the appetite ♦ The interest in biographies ♦ Ignorance of history — together with a latent sense of its growing importance

I.

We may date the appearance of a new phenomenon around 1960, in many different countries of the world. This was, and still is, the emergence of a wide and spreading interest in history, different from other waves of such interest in the past (as, for example, the one in the second half of the eighteenth century, then current mostly in certain Western European countries and among a minority of the reading classes). After 1960 an interest in history has appeared among peoples largely untouched by such in the past. It spread to many kinds of history, beyond revelations or details about their own near-present. This may be reason enough to speak of an "appetite." But whether appetite or interest, this development after 1960 was largely unprecedented. The excellent historian Margaret MacMillan called it "The History Craze" in the first chapter of her recent *Dangerous Games: The Uses and Abuses of History* (2009). "Craze" may not be quite the right word, since a craze is irrational, whereas it may be possible to recognize at least some of the reasonable sources of this development — when many people know *less* history than their forebears may have known but when *more* people are interested in history than probably ever before.

Evidences of this are so many and so protean that we should welcome a thorough study of them, well researched and laden with statistics. Here I am restricted to a far from complete listing of such evidences, particularly in the United States. In 1876, one hundred years after the Declaration of Independence, the great Centennial Exhibition in Philadelphia included a few plaster casts of the Founders, but otherwise it was almost entirely devoted to the newest products of American industrial machinery. In 1976, one hundred years later, the celebrations of the two hundredth anniversary were suffused with history on all occasions and levels. (The most spectacular of its events was a parade of old sailing ships.) This is but one example of this mutation of sentiments.

There are innumerable others. Popular historical magazines hardly existed at all before the Second World War.

There are such now in many countries of the world, in some of them at least two. Their contents are, more than often, good, reasonably accurate, many of their articles written by professional historians. The numbers of their readers and subscribers have changed not much since their inceptions. Within commercial publishing since about 1960 histories of all kinds sell better than novels. The same condition prevails for secondhand book sellers (even when there are fewer bookstores than fifty years ago). There are many history programs, history channels on television, an increasing production of historical films, "documentaries" and "docudramas," etc. What may be even more significant —because independent of publishing and of entertainment—is the growth of local historical societies, perhaps twice as many as there were fifty years ago. Their members are no longer men and women whose interest in their past is mainly genealogical. Throughout the United States the preservation of older houses and artifacts and documents has become a principal concern of such societies but also of many municipalities, rural and suburban. Many of them now have historical commissions within their governments, an inclusion rare even thirty or forty years ago. Their work is often exemplary and, as a matter of course, nonending.

Let me repeat: this is now a worldwide phenomenon. It has appeared even in portions of the world where this kind of interest, especially for relatively recent history, was rare in the past. It is especially remarkable in the United States, whose popular ethos, progressive and antiaristo-cratic, was for a long time nonhistorical. But now the historical appetites of many Americans have become un-precedented and considerable. Of course these appetites may be served, and go on being served, with plenty of junk food. Of that professional historians may be aware. Of the meaning of this appetite they are, by and large, not.

2.

Professional historians, the university and college profes-sorate, proved largely indifferent to what happened to the teaching of history in high schools. Beginning about 1970 the teaching of history in American high schools was re-duced. Around the same time the requirement of history courses was reduced or diluted in colleges and universities too. By 1980 the numbers of undergraduate history ma-jors in American institutions of higher learning had fallen to one-fourth or one-fifth what they had been twenty years earlier. Professional historians had little to do with this devolution, which was mostly the doing of admin-istrative bureaucrats and bureaucracies.

Seen from a very broad historical perspective, this was nothing very new. Two hundred years earlier the universities of France or England or Germany (though not of Scotland) or even the few colleges in the American colonies had little to do with the then democratic revolutions or even with the so-called Enlightenment. Two hundred years later the prestige of well-known historians and of their institutions was such that a concerted public effort against the dilution of the teaching of history in schools could have been halted or even reversed. But this did not happen. The personal and professional interests of most academic historians remained narrow. They paid little attention to what was happening in other schools of the nation. They should have; but they didn't.

Yet this bureaucratically promoted and managed decrease of history teaching in the schools occurred at the same time when the interests of many people in history increased. Whether the interests of masses of young people in history was increasing or not we cannot tell. There is some marginal evidence that something like the opposite prevailed, at least for a while: around 1980 many college students chose history courses among their nonrequired ones. There is also evidence that a small but remarkable minority of college students had and still have a serious interest in history, involving considerable reading on their part. Does this mean that this new phenomenon of an appetite for history has penetrated the minds of younger people too? Yes and no: for at the same time the numbers of history students and — more telling — of students choosing to go on to graduate studies in history continued to decrease. Now keep in mind that an interest in history (apart from myths and legends) often arises during a maturing of minds. Young people may be curious of this or that, but they are also docile. And, alas, so are some of their parents. In the United States the latter accepted, without questioning, the transformation of the purposes of the schools and colleges and universities that began after about 1960. Since then the mass of enrolled students kept growing and growing: but the older avowed purpose of giving them a basic liberal education has, by and large, disappeared. The goal of a college or university degree has become certification for a particular employment. Soon after 1970 the majority of students in American colleges were choosing economics or business as their professed specialty, or "major," despite the questionable value of the teaching and contents of such courses. But that is another story.

3.

History does not repeat itself. Nor do the motives and the conditions and the purposes of historical knowledge. The twentieth century was an especially transitory century, a relatively short one (1914 to 1989) but in another sense one between two historical epochs. There are many symptoms suggesting that — in many places of the world — men and women around 2000 began thinking otherwise than their forebears a century before. By this I mean not only the subjects of their thinking but the functioning of their minds: how do they employ them, and why, and when? And how does this relate to the spreading of an appetite for history?

That is a question almost impossible to answer. Perhaps we should precede our speculations by distinguishing between motives and purposes, two different things that have become, alas, often confused by lawyers, judges, psychologists, and historians. Motives push people from the past; purposes involve a pull toward a future. Motives are sometimes unconscious; purposes often, though not always, conscious. Attributing motives to people has been a frequent and deplorable and illegitimate practice during the twentieth century. Curiosity and interest are purposes rather than motives: they amount to the wish to know more about some things — also, about more history.

At the opening of the twenty-first century "people," writes Margaret MacMillan about "The History Craze," are "better educated and, particularly in the mature economies, have more leisure time and are retiring from work earlier." I am not convinced of this. It is questionable whether people are now better educated, or that they have more "leisure time." Even if this were so, it does not seem that their appetite for history exists only to fill their leisure hours. It is possible that some people find history entertaining. But then "entertainment" is too much of a vague and malleable term: isn't there an element of entertainment in searching for and then finding an object or subject of curiosity, just as pleasure is (indeed it must be) a component in the liking of reading? Another, perhaps more obvious, element in a diagnosis of the present appetite for history may be something like a curiosity compounded with anxiety: the world is changing fast around us, whence we consciously try to preserve objects from a historical past — as well as to find subjects that connect us personally with an imaginable and not so distant past. More is at work here than *nostalgia*. The original Greek phrase "nostos algos" meant a longing not for a certain *time* but for a certain *home*. Nostalgia is of course a normal human tendency, an aspiration. But it does not seem that the present interest of many kinds of people for many kinds of history is an outcome of their longing for a now gone but still more or less recent past that they themselves had known.

"Interest" is hardly separable from "curiosity" (four or five centuries ago *un curieux* in France designated someone whom we may call "an intellectual"). Curiosity and interest in details of people's recent past, including their sufferings, of course exists here and there, but it does not seem to be predominant. There is an odd time lag apparent here. It seems that for most people the knowledge of what happened to them arises not instantly or even soon after that but a considerable time later. Popular interest in the history of the Second World War, including in some of its yet unrevealed details, was not widespread during the fifteen years after the end of the war. Interest — in this case more than curiosity — about the Holocaust did not rise until the mid-1960s, especially in the United States: the very word "Holocaust" emerged and came into circulation only then; and the establishment of Holocaust museums and public remembrances in the United States was largely the work of people whose relatives had not been victims of the Holocaust. In Germany books and other works dealing with Hitler began to increase in the 1970s; studies and accounts of the massive bombing destructions of German cities not until about 2000. The sources and the conditions of the present appetites for history may be deeper than curiosity about this or that in the recent past — perhaps even deeper than the desire to acquire more knowledge. They involve the appetite for encountering some things and some people who were *real*.

One evidence of this is the change in the valuations of "old-fashioned" and "modern." In the American language as late as the 1920s "old-fashioned" was a negative adjective, while "modern" was approbatory. "An old-fashioned boy" or young man was clinging to his mother's skirts, something like a sissy; a "modern" girl was an all-American girl. (In England "modern" applied to a girl or woman suggested something racy; in the United States not.) About forty years later there was a reversal. "Old-fashioned," in America, came to suggest something respectable and solid. "Modern" had become vague and abstract, to the extent that its various meanings were now confusing.* By the 1960s an old-fashioned building, or house, or family, or restaurant, or dinner had become preferable to a "modern" one. There are many more examples of this.

This mutation has been inseparable from a probably less conscious devolution, indeed, disillusionment, with the American ideal of Progress — especially with "Progress" meaning a constant and salutary movement away from the past (and from history; and from tradition). This antihistorical mentality was of course shortsighted; but it was also a populist ideal, a basic belief not only of Progressives and liberals but of Republicans and political "conservatives," especially in the 1920s. In that politically and popularly Republican decade this American faith in

* Had the Modern Age not begun five hundred years ago, succeeding the Middle Ages? What was, and is, "modern" art or design? — something created after 1890 (and seldom applied to things after 1960 . . .)? What was (and is) "postmodern" (a word beginning to appear after 1970)? And the much touted sexual and "cultural" revolutions in the 1960s were hardly anything but repetitions of the modernity of the 1920s.

Progress was so overwhelming and near-universal that many foreign visitors to the United States observed it with dismay. Early in the 1920s Henry Ford proclaimed: "History is bunk." In the mid-1920s President Coolidge declared that the United States was unique because of its incarnation (even more than representation) of Progress. In 1928 President Hoover's secretary of commerce (Julius Klein) intoned the American faith: "Tradition is the enemy of Progress." Sixty years later most Americans would no longer speak or even think thus. And their, not always conscious, unease with "Progress" exists together with their increasing respect for and interest in history.

However — there is something like a schizophrenia observable here, perhaps especially among "conservatives" whose worship of technology exists together with their respect for traditions. During his presidency, 2001 to 2009, President George W. Bush denounced (and not once) enemies of the United States in the Middle East as "enemies of Progress." Did he believe what he was saying? Yes, he did. At the same time among American "liberals" the progressive ideology applied to many matters was not at all extinct. All of this suggests that sooner or later the great divisions now — and yet unconsciously — forming in people's minds will no longer be those of Left and Right, of "conservatives" and "liberals": but what Wendell Berry stated at the very end of the chronological twentieth century, 1999: that the great division will come, it is already latent, between men who think of themselves as creatures and men who think of themselves as machines.

4.

Looking at the shelves at the new, giant, omnium gatherum American bookstores, you will find quantities of history books; and at this time when independent small bookshops are lamentably disappearing, there are still many secondhand book dealers maintaining their businesses, many of them specializing in military histories. On their shelves and in their boxes histories and biographies are often next to each other. In the giant chain bookstores they are not: "History" and "Biography" are separated and so marked on their shelves. That is understandable and proper in some cases, but in others it is not. It depends on (a) the subject of a biography, (b) on the seriousness of its biographer.

A significant element in the general increase of interest in history is what has happened to biographies during the last thirty or forty years. Earlier during the twentieth century the literary production and consumption of biographies were declining. Biography, by and large, was accepted and categorized as a branch of literature, not of history. (The exceptions were serious and massive biographies of public political persons.) In England, too, in spite of its broad literary tradition, a biographer was one thing and a historian another. In 1932 Harold Nicolson wrote that the decline and even disappearance of biography would be forthcoming, since the scientific study of minds would replace the more or less traditional narratives of persons' lives. In 1936 Chesterton wrote very critically about biography: "Either in the best examples or the worst, one can hardly find in biography a substitute for history, or be completely satisfied by looking at the programme for the dramatis personae as an alternative to seeing the play." Nicolson and Chesterton were very different men, with very different views of the world; but both of them were wrong. The opposite has happened. During the past forty years the interest in serious biographies has grown, to such an extent that around 2000 one could speak of a golden age of biography — and this during the darkening decline of all other humanities. During the past thirty or forty years many good historians, professionals and nonprofessionals, turned their talents to writing biographies. Even more noteworthy is the condition that excellent nonacademic writers of biographies researched and relied on and employed the bibliographical standards and citational practices of nineteenth-century professional historiography. This amounted to more than the adoption of "scholarly equipment." It meant that the methods and the seriousness of biographers and of historians were no longer very different.

Carlyle said that history consists of innumerable biographies. Yes: but of numerable and available biographies first of all. The appetite for history, whether fed by histories or by biographies, is an interest in people who actually existed, therefore real. It has nothing in common with the once so fervent interest and entertainment of legends (of which "science fiction" is a present, and probably waning, excrescence). In a world of increasing (and often overwhelming and oppressing) abstractions, including the productions of ephemeral publicity, the descriptions of the lives of men and women who unquestionably and evidently existed are attractive and perhaps even inspiring.

"Man is a reed," said Pascal, "but he is a thinking reed." But: is he still a reader? The overall crisis of civilization has affected not only historianship but the availability and practice of book reading. The publishing industry, perhaps particularly in the United States, has been largely responsible for this. While publishing executives and managers have seen that many histories and biographies now sell better than many novels, they have done nothing to promote this condition. There are of course other factors of the overall decrease of a book-reading public — suburban dwelling, television, the declining standards and requirements of schools, etc. — all of these involved with a breakdown of communications, of people talking to each other about books. Still, the absorption of much of publishing by large corporations has much contributed to the decline of reading, including the reading of history. Unlike on some occasions in the past, the book-reading public has become largely docile, accepting what is easily available and what is not. There are startling examples of this.*

We must not exaggerate the meaning (or perhaps not even the evidences and the extent) of this widespread interest in history, of this new phenomenon. Will it endure? I so hope — but I dare not say. What I dare to say it that while on the stock exchange of words the recent rise of "old-fashioned" may not go on and on, the decline of "modern" will. About this I am — well, almost — certain.

---

* In the United States a pioneer in the recognition of a rising interest in history was *American Heritage* magazine, founded in 1954 by a few nonacademic historians, convinced that the writing of history must not be restricted to the circles of academic professionals. The success of *American Heritage,* its many subscribers and the quality of many of its articles, was considerable. But in the 1990s the new owners of the *American Heritage* company decided to reduce the size and transform the contents of the magazine. Soon thereafter the old *Heritage* virtually ceased to exist. So this is a counterexample of my thesis about a spreading national interest in history — while it is also an example of the shortsightedness of corporate owners and managers obsessed with "the bottom line" (or, more accurately: with quick profits).

5.

There is — unfortunately — no sign that the recent interest in history has had considerable effects on the politics and the politicians of the present. They speak in favor and vote in support of historical preservations, anniversaries, and commemorations of many kinds. But: do they know more history than their political forebears knew? It does not seem so. The functions of human knowledge are such that the more knowledge a man has of something the easier it is for him to accumulate more knowledge about and around it. There is not much evidence that politicians' interest in history is growing. Of course there are individual exceptions to this. But present-mindedness rather than past-mindedness is a standard inclination of democratic politicians, and also of the governors of large governmental institutions. Sometimes their ignorance of important and relevant historical events is (or should be) remarkable. Condoleezza Rice was the secretary of state and the main foreign policy adviser in George W. Bush's administration, a woman with a doctor's degree in international relations, and a recognized expert on matters of the Cold War and the Soviet Union. In 2004 or 2005 she admitted that she did not know that Turkey as well as Greece was included in the so-called Truman doctrine in 1947, which was the first American military commitment at the start of the Cold War. No one noticed this evidence of her ignorance, though they should have.

The thoughtless, though sometimes instinctive, acceptance of dubious facts and legends is frequent among politicians, now especially among those of the present Eastern European states well after their emancipation from Soviet and/or Communist sovereignty. Misconceptions, misperceptions, and misuses of history have always existed, here and there current even in the more traditional democracies of the West. One recent — and, by now, long-lived and frequent — example is the citing of Munich 1938 by politicians, warning of what would happen if and when an illegitimate compromise or concession to a dangerous dictator is being considered. But what happened in Munich in 1938, less than one year before the outbreak of the Second World War, involving Hitler and Chamberlain, is not applicable when facing an Asian or Middle Eastern or even Russian dictator, whether in the 1950s or fifty years later. History does not repeat itself,* even when historical circumstances seem to.

Misconceptions and, consequently, wrong presenta-

---

* Besides, we know (or ought to know) now that Hitler was not bluffing in Munich; that his opponents were much less prepared (or ready) to fight him then than a year later; that Stalin's Soviet Union would not have joined them. Etc., etc.

tions of this or that historical event will always happen, affecting the histories of entire peoples on occasion. But our anxiety here is something different: it concerns appetite, not nutrition. Will the current appetite for history eventually bring about a deepening of historical understanding—even when the actual teaching of history has been diminishing? Well—with all of the somber evidences to the contrary—I at least hope so. Consciously or not, more people seem to be aware of the truth in Cicero's epigram: "To be ignorant of what happened before you were born is to remain a child always." Puerility may be rampant, marking some of the words and even gestures* of American presidents, but they will not last. Nearly a century ago the American essayist Agnes Repplier wrote: "I used to think that ignorance of history meant only a lack of cultivation and a loss of pleasure. [Yes, pleasure!] Now I'm sure that such ignorance impairs our judgment by impairing our understanding, by depriving us of standards of the power of contrast, and the right to estimate. . . . We can know nothing of any nation unless we know its history." Since then something less obvious but also profound has been emerging. Around 1980 the extraordinary English thinker Owen Barfield wrote:

---

* E.g., the liking of our "conservative" presidents, Reagan and the younger Bush, for playing soldier: saluting with their bare hands, etc.

The Western outlook emphasizes the importance of history and pays ever increasing attention to it. . . . There is a new concept of *history* in the air, a new feeling for its true significance. We have witnessed the dim dawning of a sense that history is to be grasped as something substantial in the being of man, as an "existential encounter."

That "dawning" may be dim, but it is there. And the present appetite for history, whatever its excrescences, is only a part of it.

FOUR

Re-Cognition of History as Literature

History, including its facts, consists of words ♦ Absurdities of "social history" while history is literature ♦ "Amateur" historians and their merits ♦ Neither "objective" nor "subjective" but "participant" ♦ Historical idealism is not categorical or determinist. The decisive significance of "when?"

I.

History; is it art or science? "History is an art, like the other sciences"; a felicitous paradoxical epigram crafted by Veronica Wedgwood, a very erudite and charmingly modest English historian, not inclined to produce epigrams. Here my question is somewhat different. Is the writing of history literary or scientific? Is history literature or science? Well—it *is* literature rather than science. And so it should be. For us.

In the eighteenth century Veronica Wedgwood's epigram would have been a truism, since in that century people did not regard the difference between art and science that is obvious for us. We have seen that during that time they saw history as a branch of literature. But we do not and cannot return to the eighteenth century. Our consideration of history is not a return to history as literature but a — somewhat — new recognition.

The emphasis is on letters and words. Let us imagine that at some future time the printed word may cease to exist (except in remnant books or microfilms or other reprintable devices). Will then a film, or any other series of pictures, reconstructing — or, rather, confecting — a then recent or past historical episode amount to authentic history? No: because it will be a necessarily complicated technical construction. History writing (and teaching) are reconstructions too: but their sources are authentic, from men and women who really lived, their acts and words being *retold* but not *reenacted*. And described and told in a common and everyday language, comprehensible to their writers and teachers as well as to their readers. History writing does not depict: it describes.

In the beginning was the word: and then the letter; and then literature. Does history consist of Facts? Yes, there are "facts." The house was burning. The dog did not bark. Julius Caesar crossed the Rubicon. Napoleon lost at Waterloo. But "facts" have four limitations at least. One: for us the meaning of every fact exists because of our instant association and comparison of it with other facts. Two: for us the meaning of every fact depends on its statement, on the words with which it is expressed. Three: these words depend on their purposes. There are statements in which the "fact" may be true, but the meaning, the tendency, the purpose of its statement may be false.* Fourth: "fact" has its history too. Five or more centuries ago the word "fact" (as also such words as "objective" and "subjective") meant not what they now mean or are assumed or pretend to mean. Fact meant "feat," something done.

Words are not finite categories but meanings: what they mean to us, for us. They have their own histories and lives and deaths, their powers and their limits. Let us imagine (it is not easy, but imaginable) that at some future time human beings may communicate with each other entirely by pictures, images, numbers, codes. When words will cease to exist, people will not: but their consciousness of history, including their own history, will.

2.

At this late date the recognition that history is literature, rather than science, runs against the determinable in-

---

* Blake: "A Truth that's told with bad intent / Beats all the Lies you can invent."

clination to render history ever more "scientific" — all-encompassing, useful, concrete.* The realization (which is not a re-cognition) that the historian must deal with subjects wider and deeper than the records of states and of governments and powers, with more and more people, has led to all kinds of erudite explorations, including social history at its best, but also at its worst. A move in the former direction was the French *Annales* school, with superb historians such as Marc Bloch (killed during World War II in 1944) and some of his colleagues and successors producing valuable representations of small as well as large subjects ever since. But now read what the highly reputed French historian Lucien Febvre, once a colleague and then a successor to Bloch, wrote at the acme of his career, in 1949:

> Like all the sciences history is now evolving rapidly. Certain men are increasingly endeavouring, hesitating and stumbling as they do so, to move in the direction of team work. The day will come when people will talk about "history laboratories" as real things. . . . One or two generations ago the historian was an old gentleman sitting in his armchair in front of his index cards which were strictly reserved for his

---

* About the different meanings of "science" and "scientific" in different languages and in different times see above, pages 6–7n.

own personal use and as jealously protected against envious rivals as a portfolio in a strongbox; but Anatole France's old gentleman and all those described by so many others have come to the end of their curious lives. They have given way to the alert and flexible research director who, having received a very broad education, having been trained to seek in history material with which to look for solutions to the great problems of life which societies and civilizations come up against daily, will be able to map out any investigation, put the right questions, point to precise sources of information, and, having done that, estimate expenditure, control the rotation of equipment, establish the number of staff in each team and launch his workers into a search for the unknown. . . . In a word we shall have to approach things on a far larger scale.*

Well — this was (and is) not what happened. During the past sixty years much excellent history has been written and is still being written not by teams but by individual men and women (and by "professionals" as well as "amateurs"), some of them using a computer and yes, many of them their index cards. So much for Lucien Febvre and his

*A New Kind of History: From the Writings of Febvre, ed. Peter Burke, trans. K. Folca (New York, 1973), 32–33.

"new kind of history"—as, too, for Fernand Braudel and his "total history." Learned historians they, and not devoid of imagination: but, as the French bon mot puts it, *faux bonhommes,* not *quite* good men . . .

However: they are not our problem. That problem is that the broadening of historians' perspectives so often led not to a deepening but to a shallowing of their craft. "Social" (and "gender," "economic," "religious," "intellectual," "sexual") histories are now manifold and rampant. Here is a—*very* random—list of articles and books recently published and reviewed in the *American Historical Review:*

"The Foreign Policy of the Calorie" (Cullather),
    April 2007
"Clockwatchers and Stargazers: Time Discipline in
    Early Modern Berlin" (Sautner), June 2007
"Big Hair: A Wig History of Consumption in 18th
    Century France" (Kwass), June 2006
"The Discomforts of Drag: (Trans) Gender
    Performance Among Prisoners of War in Russia"
    (Rachmaninov), April 2006
"Picturing Grief: Soviet Holocaust Photography at
    the Intersection of History and Memory"
    (Shneer), 2010
"From 'Black Rice' to 'Brown': Rethinking the

History of Risiculture and the Seventeenth and
Eighteenth Century Atlantic" (Hawthorne),
February 2010

"Thinking Sex in the Transnational Turn"
(Canaday), December 2009

"Latin America and the Challenge of Globalizing
the History of Sexuality" (Sigal), December 2009

"The Triumph of the Egg" (Freidberg), Annual
Article Award, The Berkshire Conference of
Women Historians, 2008

"Eye Appeal: The Politics of Sexual Looking in a
Consumer Society" (Lindsley), winner of the
Aldon Duane Bell Award in Women's History,
University of Washington, 2008

"Orgasm in the West: A History of Pleasure from
the Sixteenth Century to the Present" (Muchem-
bled), 2009. Reviewed by James R. Farr: "This is
a bold book by a great historian."

Alas! These titles need no further comment. Alas! They
are not untypical. They prove how low much of professional historianship, searching for subjects, has now sunk.

But what must shock us involves more than the selection
of such subjects. What are the sources for these kinds
of topics? What are their evidences? The latter are, prac-
tically without exceptions, insufficient and inconsequential.

Jacques Barzun said in the 1970s that the current practices of social history are hardly anything more than retrospective sociology. Now let me add that they are, often, not even that. Sociology, with all of its limitations, can be serious and valuable: an exhaustive (and sometimes comprehensive) study of a society or of a definite portion of it. But the above-listed examples are not that. They are attempts at a scientific sociography (which is almost a contradiction in itself). The aim of sociology is definition. The aim of sociography is description — whence it is, inevitably, literary and historical.

Literary, rather than "scientific." There is an — at least partial — concordance here between history and the novel (a relationship which the next chapter of this book shall address). Just about every novel is sociographical; it tells us things about people and their society in a certain place at a certain time. Not every history is sociographical: not every historical subject does necessarily include the description of a society of a certain time. But *description* is what they have in common. ("Description," even more than mere "narrative.") A choice of words, phrases, sentences, nouns as well as adjectives or adverbs, of significances and sequences, of meanings: choices that are more than stylistic — they are moral. There may be a moral purpose behind a scientific statement, but there is nothing that is moral or immoral in its mathematic accuracy. But the purpose of history is understanding even more than accuracy (though not without a creditable respect for the latter).

And this is at least one reason why historians ought to read literature, and even more than statistics: to truly widen and deepen their acquaintance with their chosen subject, but also to recognize that their main task is a kind of literature, rather than a kind of science. The converse of this desideratum has been stated recently by the Polish poet Adam Zagajewski:

> I am not a historian, but I'd like literature to assume, consciously and in all seriousness, the function of a historical chronicle. I don't want it to follow the example set by modern historians, cold fish by and large, who spend their lives in vanquished archives and write in an inhuman, ugly, wooden, bureaucratic language from which all poetry's been driven, a language flat as a wood louse and petty as the daily paper. I'd like it to return to earlier examples, maybe even Greek, to the ideal of the historian-poet, a person who either has seen and experienced what he describes for himself, or has drawn upon a living oral tradition, his family's or his tribe's, who doesn't fear engagement and emotion, but who cares nonetheless about his story's truthfulness.

"His story's truthfulness." Ah! there the dog lies buried. (And there too the dangers lie.)

Yes, the state of academic history writing is bad, though not quite how this good Polish poet states it. There are still many historians (with their index cards). Zagajewski's exhortation is: "Literature! Writers! Get into, get with history!" My exhortation is the reverse: Historians! Get into, get with literature!

3.

Well-written history is still being produced (and will be produced) by professional historians. More well-written history is, and will be, produced by "amateur," that is, nonprofessional historians. Because of this I must sum up something about the relationship of "professionals" and "amateurs" writing history.

Some things ought to be obvious. The distinction between professionals and amateurs writing history may exist, but it makes less sense than it does in other disciplines. A professional brain surgeon should perform a brain operation, an amateur not. But to say that a poet must have a Ph.D. in poetry is an absurdity. To say that a historian must have a Ph.D. in history is not an absurdity, but somehow in between the case of the brain surgeon and that of the poet. The other, related but also obvious, matter is that "amateur," that is, nonprofessional, nonacademic, noncertified historians have often produced excellent, on occasion magisterial books, better than those written by professionals about the same or related subjects. So we may go as far as to state that when it comes to history writing (and also to historical research), a distinction between professionals and nonprofessionals may exist, but it does not amount to a categorical difference.

After all, the instrument of their craft is the same: everyday language. We have seen that in England the literary tradition lasted longer, and the consideration of history as a science came somewhat reluctantly later than in most other countries. But during the twentieth century the relationship between academic and nonacademic historians became more complicated, even in England. Professional historians have been (and often are) jealous of the public success of their amateur confrères, while nonprofessionals, on occasion, reveal a, sometimes uneasy, respect for established professionals.* Yet in some countries, Austria,

* One example: Churchill — not a modest writer — in the preface of his *The Second World War:* "I do not describe [my record] as history, for that belongs to another generation. But I claim with confidence that it is a contribution to history which will be of service for the future." Well — Churchill (as in some of his other books) was something more than a categorizable "amateur." (At the very time I am writing this chapter, I am reading *Winston's War, 1940–1945* by Max Hastings, on the same tremendous subject: it is first-class, a worthy companion to Churchill's own six volumes — and, again, not written by an academic.)

for example, histories about the first half of the twentieth century, and especially about Hitler, are by such master historians as Friedrich Heer and Brigitte Hamann, who have had no academic appointment. (Hitler remains a particular case. Of the almost one thousand books and biographies written about him, the best are not by professional historians,* including even the excellent and conscientious Ian Kershaw.)

There are reasons for this. One is that "amateur" historians are often more literary than are their academic competitors. (In so many instances their love for literature led them to history, whereas for many academics their interest in history may lead them to consider, here and there, literature—but not necessarily so: their main interest may still be the reading of the works of other professionals.) Another reason (or, rather, condition) is that some amateurs may know more of the world—including human types—than do professionals, ever so often confining their lives within their academic circles. Here is an example that, in a moment, struck me like a splendid spark. In the second volume of his magisterial work about the Franco-Russian alliance of 1894 (*The Fateful Alliance: France, Russia, and the Coming of the First World War,* 1984), George Kennan described the chief of the French Army Staff, General Bois-

---

* About this see my *The Hitler of History,* 1997.

deffre, better than Boisdeffre's portrait limned by no lesser novelist than Marcel Proust in *Jean Santeuil.* The latter was not at all a book about the Franco-Russian alliance: but Kennan read it.*

Historians: please hear what Jacob Burckhardt told his (few) students in Basel: that history has really no method, but you must know how to read. (What; how; and when.) Three hundred years ago Lady Mary Wortley Montagu: "No entertainment is as cheap as reading, nor any pleasure so lasting." (The first part of this sentence is no longer so [television; movies] — the second yes.)†

In 1932 Christopher Dawson replied to Alan Bullock

---

* "How many professional historians are there who would so modestly, so elegantly, and so knowledgeably include a portrait by a novelist at the outset of your book? Hardly any." (My letter to Kennan, 18 February 1990.) "My own efforts to write diplomatic history taught me that there is no such thing as an objective historical reality outside 'the eye of the beholder' — none, at least, that would be accessible to the human understanding — there is only the view taken of it by the individual historian, the value of which varies with the qualities — the honesty, the scrupulousness, the imagination, and the capacity for empathy — of the historian himself. This is why I view every work of narrative history as a work of the creative imagination, like the novel, but serving a somewhat different purpose and responsive to different, more confining rules." (Letter by Kennan to me, 27 July 1984.)

† One hundred fifty years ago, Trollope (in *The Claverings*): "As for reading . . . men and women believe the work is, to be, of all works, the easiest. . . . Alas, if the habit be not there, of all tasks it is the most difficult. If a man has not acquired the habit of reading till he be old, he shall sooner in his old age learn to make shoes than learn the adequate use of a book."

(in "The Problem of Metahistory"), "The academic historian is perfectly right in insisting on the techniques of historical criticism and research. But the mastery of these techniques will not produce great history, any more than a mastery of metrical technique will produce great poetry." "Bisogna saper leggere": poetry, anecdotes, jokes, all kinds of stories may help to understand a past.*

So historians must read and know what to read—a knowledge and interest and, yes, an appetite that will not only enrich their minds but guide and inspire their writing. In the long sad history of mankind we know of a few genius poets and writers who read little. But good historians? No. Yet I know many historians who have deprived their minds *and* their research of their topics by ignoring the literature of that period. An acquaintance of mine whose main professional interest was British liberal politics in the 1960s consistently refused to read Trollope. Another acquaintance whose "field" was the Enlightenment did not read Tocqueville's *Old Regime and the French Revolution*.

---

* Max Beerbohm wrote this epigrammatic witticism about the 1880s: "To give an accurate and exhaustive account of that period would need a far less brilliant pen than mine." (A rare example of a good half-truth.) About the 1890s the American essayist and amateur historian Thomas Beer in his *The Mauve Decade,* incarnating an insatiable and intelligent curiosity, knew not only how but what to read, whence the unusual quality of his book.

Tocqueville is a good case in point. The occasional rec-ognition of what he (and successfully) in the *Ancient Re-gime* attempted, that in his research and evidences his go-ing beneath the colorful surface of events was something profound and new, was made by French literary critics, not historians. There has been evolution here: but even now Tocqueville is classified as a social and political thinker, rather than a historian. Or consider his brilliant memoir of the 1848 revolutions (originally written only for himself, and then discovered by a nephew forty years later in a desk). These recollections of 1848 are exceptional in their perspicacity and style.

What happened, and what people then thought and per-haps still think happened, may be found in a variety of sources, in some places (and times) hidden, in others not. To search for them is, or should be, the unavoidable duty of serious professional historians. And even those among them who respect literature must understand that the qual-ity (and even the style) of writing is more than a matter of literary technique. A historian (and a good one) once said to me that, yes, historians often refrain from employing adjectives that could enliven their narrative accounts. True —even though the mark of good writing resides less in adjectives than in verbs. (James Joyce in *Dubliners:* "She sat at the window, watching the evening invade the avenue.")

For an honest historian his duty includes, involves both

writing and teaching — even when he is not speaking in a classroom. He also ought to know that the relationship between the spoken and the written word is not simple. Speech, contrary to Freud's doctrine (and perhaps also to Joyce's idea in *Ulysses*), is more than an outcome of thought: it is the realization of it. When it comes to writing I cannot but agree with T.S. Eliot — that the motive to write is the desire to vanquish a mental preoccupation by expressing it consciously and clearly. But in speaking as well as in writing, the choice of every word is not only an esthetic or a technical but a moral choice. Of this historians ought to be even more aware than are other writers in other professions.

4.

There is much that historians have yet to learn. Especially now when the chaotic crisis in all kinds of disciplines — indeed, of civilization itself — has reached the historical profession. They have to confront the conditions of their knowledge — indeed, of all human knowledge — for the sake of the health and the future of their discipline. For now, at the end of an age, when the concept and the ideal of Objectivity have faded, there are new dangers already apparent. One of them is Subjectivity (involved with "postmodernism").

If knowledge of the past (again, like all kinds of human knowledge) is *participant,* is that designation not necessarily *subjective?* It is not: because Subjectivism, as also Objectivism, tends to be (and often actually is) determinist. Earlier in this book I suggested that the cultural and civilizational crisis seems to have reached the historical profession around 1960, a necessarily inaccurate dating: but it may be significant that 1961 was the publication date of *What Is History?* by Edward Hallett Carr (his Trevelyan Lectures), a book that, we are told, has sold hundreds of thousands of copies since then. Forty years later there was a symposium commemorating Carr's book, held at the Institute of Historical Research in London. *What Is History?* is "the classic we celebrate and commemorate," said and wrote one of the speakers (Professor Linda Colley). Another contributor (Professor Alice Kessler-Harris): "My generation of graduate students in the U.S. cut their teeth on E. H. Carr." (Much orthodontic treatment still needed.) And what did Carr pronounce? "Before you study the history, study the historian." According to Carr the historian's background — especially his social background — virtually determines the history he writes. Well — how about some of the sons (and daughters) of rich bourgeois who became Marxists; or the offsprings of Jewish Marxists who chose to become conservatives? In any event — by 1961 the once rigidly economic (and pro-Soviet) determinist Carr moved, or slid, into another version of determinism, a subjectivist one.* (Consider that subjective determinism was also the essence of Adolf Hitler's convictions about human nature: "Jews can only think in a Jewish way." His idealist determinism: "We will win because our ideas are stronger and better than those of our opponents." Otherwise history makes no sense.)

And—an important "and" for us—still Carr kept on insisting that history was, and is, A Science. He could not free himself from the Objective-Subjective terminology. In *What Is History?* he wrote: "It does not follow that, because a mountain appears to take on different angles of vision, it has *objectively* [my italics] no shape at all, or an infinity of shapes." But the more "objective" our concept of the shape of the mountain, the more abstract that mountain becomes. Even more important, historically: the existence of the mountain was meaningless until men appeared, and then saw it; and eventually called it "a mountain," different from other protuberances. Much, much later did someone conceive it as an "objective fact."

In sum: perspective is an—inevitable—component of

---

* Dabblers in the history of ideas should note that Carr's book of 1961 nearly coincided with Thomas Kuhn's *The Structure of Scientific Revolutions,* 1962, a worthless book in which vocabulary substitutes for thought, and which slides into Subjectivism, though it does not quite dare to espouse it while suggesting that science is but the result of scientists, the result "of a consensus of the scientific community."

reality. In sum: participation is the — inevitable — insepar-ability of the knower from the known. There is now a corresponding recognition of this condition in physics, too: that the "subject" of the search or re-search of sub-atomic matter is not matter "itself" but the physicist's investigation of matter. Many physicists are unwilling to think about this, just as many historians are unwilling to think about the limitations of their "objectivity." Is the latter an acknowledgment of human limitations? Yes, it is: yet it is the kind of acknowledgment that does not reduce but enriches the functioning and the qualities of our minds.*

The future of history lies there. The knower and the known are not identical: but they are inseparable. That is,

* Participation involves memory; and also inspiration. Huizinga: "There is in our historical consciousness an element of great importance that is best defined by the term historical sensation. One might also call it histor-ical contact. . . . This contact with the past, a contact which it is impossible to determine or analyse completely . . . is one of the many ways given to man to reach beyond himself, to experience truth. The object of this feeling is not people as individuals. . . . It is hardly an image which our minds forms. . . . It if takes on a form at all this remains composite and vague: an *Ahnung* [sense] of streets, houses, as sounds and colours or people moving or being moved. There is in this manner of contact with the past the absolute conviction of reality. . . . The historical sensation is not the sensation of living the past again but of understanding the world as one does when listening to music." (*The Task of Cultural History,* VII, 71). Professor Kossmann at the Huizinga centennial conference, 1972: "I find it difficult to understand what exactly Huizinga was trying to describe in these passages." I don't.

too, how we, on this earth, are at the center of the universe. We did not create the universe; but we invented it, and keep inventing it, time after time.

Our knowledge of history is of course less than the entire past, but it is also more than the recorded past. But the remembered past is also incomplete, and fallible, and ever changing. Memory brings something from a past into a present; it is a function not unique to human beings. But while we are not only responsible for what we think, we are responsible, too, for what we remember — or, more precisely: what we choose to remember. (And memory has its history, too: a famous passage from Dante: "Nothing is more miserable than remembering good times in times of woe." Many of us, in the twentieth century, remember that such memories could be sustaining.)

5.

The historian's choice of his subject is governed by his interests. But what kinds of interests? Looking at some of the recent subjects chosen by professional historians, recognizing the absurdity of some of them, already involves a question: what was the essence of their interest? how did they become interested in their subject? were they really inspired by their choice? "How" and "really" — was their interest more or less authentic? or was their choice the outcome of a personal concern involving their professional careers? The unavoidable relationship of the knower with the known does not mean that the knower and the known are identical — nor is the character of a historian and the worth of his subject.

When, say, three hundred years ago an early frost destroyed a peasant's crops, this change in his material conditions during a then cruel winter meant very much. But what was he thinking? We (unlike God) may know little or nothing about that. In any event: did his thinking affect the material state of his existence? Perhaps not much. In our mass democratic age conditions are different. The value of everything, material as well as intellectual or spiritual, is what people think it is. That has always been so, at least to some extent; but less than it has become. (This is what I have dared to call a mental intrusion into the structure of events — we may even go so far as to call it an increasing spiritualization [and abstraction] of matter.) This of course runs against the accepted belief that we now live in an overwhelmingly materialistic world, and that people are overwhelmingly materialistic. Yet what people — whether individual persons or masses of people — think is the fundamental essence of what happens in this world, the material products and institutions of it being the consequences, indeed the superstructures. And what people think and believe — and what people thought and believed—are matters (yes: matters) that, all of their documented evidences notwithstanding, are difficult to trace. (And, in re-searching such matters, literature may be a better guide than science.)

This is not a proposition of categorical idealism. Ideas and beliefs are not abstractions, they are historical, like everything human. But they are not the obvious outcomes of some kind of a *Zeitgeist*. I repeat: recognize that people do not *have* ideas. They choose them. (And how, or why, and when they choose?—difficult questions these.) Here is my disagreement with the neo-idealist R. G. Collingwood, who—a subjectivist determinist—recognizing that a German historian who was born in 1900 would see the past differently from a French historian who was born in 1800, concludes: "There is no point in asking which was the right point of view. Each was the only one possible for the man who adopted it." *The only one possible?* That French historian born in 1800 could have been a monarchist, or a republican, or a Bonapartist; a Germanophile or a Germanophobe—that German historian born in 1900 could have been a conservative or a liberal; a Francophobe or a Francophile. And so about the subjects of their interests: it is at least imaginable that a German historian born in 1900 could prefer to read and write about Louis XIV, or that a French historian born in 1800 about Friedrich Wilhelm I. There is the perennial condition that people will tend to adjust their ideas to circumstances (or: what they think those circumstances are), rather than adjust circumstances to their ideas. One large consequence of this is the slow change of movements of political beliefs. Again—entirely contrary to Marx et al.—these movements are seldom the results of material conditions. What marks the movements in the history of societies and peoples is not the accumulation of capital. It is the accumulation of opinions. (And such accumulations can be promoted, and for some time even produced, by manipulations of publicity, confected for the majority by hard small minorities—though not always, and not forever.)

Beyond and beneath the difficult task of reconstructing what people thought, and of the growing influence of mind into matter, is the phenomenon of inflation, another fundamentally democratic development. When there is more and more of something, it tends to be worth less and less. Consider, if only for a moment, the now virtual disappearance of the once inflation-deflation "business cycles." What we now have is a constant inflation, though at varying speeds. And the inflation of words and slogans, of categories and standards, of pictures and images led to the inflation of money and of possessions, not the other way around. Consider the dematerialization of money and of other possessions, especially in nations where creditability (a potential) has become more important than are actual possessions (that may be legally "owned" but are, in reality, rented). This, often dangerous and also artificial, spiritualization of matter has led to more and more abstractions influencing people. (And here again, consider once more the benefices of literature — which, when good, abhors an inflation of words.)

But this intrusion of minds into the structure of events renders description more and more difficult: because, no matter how much information is available about them, "simple" people are no longer very simple. And, of course, neither are educated ones. When reading Dickens or Balzac, Thackeray or Flaubert, Trollope or Conrad or *Buddenbrooks,* we learn easily not only *what* but *how* Gradgrind or Goriot's daughters or Becky Sharp or Charles Bovary or Dr. Grantly or Kurtz or "Toni" Buddenbrook, whether major or minor characters, were thinking, how they used their minds. About a man or woman living in New York in 2011 — what is, what may be going on in their minds? No simple attribution will do. Or: was Dwight D. Eisenhower a simpler man than was Ulysses S. Grant? He was not.

And so a thoughtful historian must direct his attention not only to *what* ideas have been current but to *how* and *why* they had arisen and then invaded and even changed the histories of peoples. And to this he must add the very historical question: *when?* Again it was Kierkegaard who uttered a profound and yet commonsensical truth: "It is possible to be *both* good and bad, but it is impossible *at one and the same time* to become both good and bad." (This amounts to more even than another truthful maxim about human nature crafted by La Rochefoucauld: "There are evil men who would be less dangerous were it not that they have something good in them too.") Kierkegaard's statement is about God's creation of *time*. It is also an answer to the uneasy question of some people about someone like Hitler. Fourteen years ago (in *The Hitler of History,* 43–44) I wrote: "Yes, there was plenty of evil in Hitler's expressed thoughts, wishes, thoughts, statements, and decisions. (I emphasize *expressed,* since that is what evidence properly allows us to consider.) But keep in mind that evil as well as good is part of human nature. Our inclinations to evil (whether they mature into acts or not) are reprehensible but also normal. To deny that human condition leads us to the assertion that Hitler was abnormal; and the simplistic affixing of the "abnormal" label to Hitler relieves him, again, of responsibility — indeed, categorically so."* The

* "It is not only that Hitler had considerable intellectual talents. He was also courageous, self-assured, on many occasions steadfast, loyal to his friends and to those working for him, self-disciplined and modest in his physical wants. What this suggests ought not be misconstrued, mistaken, or misread. It does not mean: lo and behold! Hitler was only 50 percent bad. Human nature is not like that. A half-truth is worse than a lie, because a half-truth is not a 50 percent truth: it is a 100 percent truth and a 100 percent untruth mixed together. In mathematics, with its rigidly fixed and immobile numbers, 100 plus 100 makes

Hitler who was kind to children and to his dog and the Hitler who wished and ordered the elimination of entire peoples was the same person, at different times.

When? All prose literature is concerned with *when?* Earlier I wrote that a fact is inseparable from its statement, and that its statement is hardly separable from its purpose, and that the purpose of historians should be the reduction of untruths. In 1994 I also wrote: "I must now add something to this: [There is] the inevitable historicity — which does not mean the relativity — of human truth. To say 'A black man is as good as any of you' at a Ku Klux Klan Konklave in 1915 is something quite different from saying the same words to a liberal audience in 1970. To say (and not merely mutter): "A German Jew is worth more than a Viennese Nazi" in a crowded Munich streetcar in 1942 is something very different from pronouncing the same words at an anti-Nazi rally in New York in 1942 (or to a Berlin audience in, say, 1972). This is obvious. But I am not speaking merely of different kinds of courage. I am attempting to suggest that the statement at the Ku Klux Klan rally in 1915 or the statement in the Munich streetcar in 1942 may not have been entire truths, but somehow

---

200; in human life 100 plus 100 makes *another* kind of 100. Life is not constant: it is full of black 100s and white 100s, warm 100s and cold 100s, 100s that are growing and 100s that are shrinking" (43–44).

truer than the same statements at another time and in another place. Because they were exceptional. And in history — more than in science — exceptions do matter.

Every good novelist knows this. So should every good historian.

FIVE

History and the Novel

Historians and novelists. Different tasks ♦ "Fact" and "fiction"
♦ The origins and the history of the novel, which historians
must consider ♦ Every novel is a historical novel ♦ Potentiality:
What happened; what might have happened ♦ Recent and current crisis of the novel ♦ Absorption of the novel by history: A
new form of literature ♦ A small addendum

I.

"History," Macaulay once wrote, "begins in novel and
ends in essay." This is a terse maxim. What does it mean?
The historian, like the novelist, tells a story; a story of
some portion of the past; he describes (rather than de-
fines). The novelist has it easier: he can invent people who
did not exist and events that did not happen. The historian cannot describe people and events that did not exist;
he must limit himself to men and women who really lived;
he must depend on evidences of their acts and words —
though, like the novelist, he too must surmise something

about their minds. In one word: to *essay* — a word that is close to "assay" but is more than that: not only weighing the evidence but attempting to find its meaning. Historians must be capable — and willing — to do that. But do they understand that some kind of a moral is inherent in *every* human event, and in every human expression? There are not many historians whose view of history, by and large, includes their task to promote historical thinking. Such historians are teachers, perhaps even more than writers: they teach, too, when they write. Do novelists teach when they write? Seldom: when and if they do so, that teaching is implicit.

Mencken said in a quip that the historian is a frustrated novelist; but one must read Tolstoy to find, rather, that the novelist may be a frustrated historian. It is easier to write a mediocre history than a mediocre novel. It is more difficult to write a great history than a great novel. This is why, in the past two hundred years, there may have been more great novels than great histories. "A great historian," Macaulay wrote, "would reclaim those materials which the novelist has appropriated." And: "To be a really great historian is perhaps the rarest of intellectual distinctions." But it is not as simple as that.

2.

History has two definitions, the novel has one. Did history exist before historians, does it exist without its recorders and narrators? It did and it does.* Can a novel exist without a novelist, without its writer? It cannot. This distinction is commonsensical; but it is also incomplete. A juxtaposition of the historian and the novelist as categorical opposites is not absolute. Neither is the categorical juxtaposition of "fact" and "fiction." "Fiction" means construction, whence there is some "fiction" in the statement (and even in the perception) of every "fact."

History is unavoidably anthropocentric: it consists of the knowledge that human beings have of other human beings. That knowledge involves all of our senses, including seeing: and seeing involves thinking and imagination, the latter amounting to construction, too, with a bit of will in it.†

* "Pre-history," therefore, is a nonsensical category. In 1871 the *O.E.D.* defined it as "the account of events or conditions prior to written or recorded history." But human history existed before it was recorded or written.

† To this we may add that there is ample evidence that different people, in different times and in different places, did not entirely *see* the way we are accustomed to seeing. They used their eyes otherwise because their imagination came forth otherwise. (See the exceptionally intelligent book by a young American art historian, Samuel Y. Edgerton Jr., in *The Renaissance Rediscovery of Linear Perspective*, 1975.

In *Elective Affinities* (*Die Wahlverwandtschaften*) Goethe wrote: "We may imagine ourselves in any situation we like, but we always think of ourselves as seeing. [Even] in dreams we can not stop seeing. Someday

Fact and Fiction are related to each other. But identical they are not. (And notwithstanding the limitations of a "fact," it is a principal duty of every historian to correct imprecise or untrue "facts" stated by others.) Yet: if every fact is, to some extent, a fiction; if the historian must be master of his words even more than of his facts — is there anything left to distinguish him from a novelist? Let me assure my historian confrères: they have nothing to fear. The difference between the historian and the novelist exists. My argument implies not the fictional nature of history; it suggests, instead, the historicity of fiction. And that happened because of the rise of historical consciousness, because historical thinking affected novelists even more profoundly than the novel has affected historians.

3.

The novel, like professional history, was a product of the eighteenth century. It may have had a few odd forerunners, but the modern novel appeared about 1750. It was a new form of literature. Other branches of literature are about three thousand years old, but the novel was a mod-

---

perhaps the inner light will shine forth from us, and then we shall need no other light." The great historian Burckhardt: "Unser Auge ist sonnenhaft, sonst sähe es die Sonne nicht." Our eye is sunlike: otherwise the sun it could not see.

ern phenomenon. People thought, and many still do, that the novel, being narrative, is a prose form of the epic. They were, and are, mistaken. "The novel and the epic," wrote Ortega y Gasset in 1914,

> are precisely poles apart. The theme of the epic is the past as such: it speaks to us about a world which was and which is no longer, of a mythical age whose antiquity is not a past in the same sense as any remote historical time. It is true that local piety kept gradually linking Homeric men and gods to the citizens of the present by means of slender threads, but this net of genealogical traditions does not succeed in bridging the absolute gap which exists between the mythical *yesterday* and the real *today*. No matter how many real yesterdays we interpolate, the sphere inhabited by the Achilleses and the Agamemnons has no relationship with our existence and we cannot reach it, step by step, by retracing the path opened up by the march of time. The epic past is not *our* past. Our past is thinkable as having been the present once, but the epic past eludes identification with any possible present. . . . No, it is not a remembered past, but an ideal past.

The success of the novel, which soon became the dominant form of literature, was largely due to the condition that its readers could identify themselves with the novel's actors, scenes, problems, times. We may therefore say that the novel belonged to the bourgeois age, that it was a bourgeois genre of literature. (And, as we shall see, the current troubles and the possible demise of the novel may also be one result of the passing of the bourgeois age and of bourgeois societies.) Meanwhile professional history, despite all of its present troubles, may not disappear with the bourgeois age.

But historians of the past two hundred years should have, and ought to, consider some of its novels seriously, for more than one reason. There are at least four ways in which novelists have produced valuable evidences for historians. First: novelists furnished actual historical materials: vivid details about certain pasts, many of them historically verifiable, since the novelist's interests may be often comparable to the historian's. Moreover, the novelist, through his art of selecting, ordering, and describing such details, may draw the historian's attention to "overlooked" aspects, scenes, problems, even periods. The classic examples are Scott, Balzac, certain books of Dickens. Many historians have respected Scott's merits. Balzac's *Comédie Humaine,* taking place between 1792 and 1840, is chock full of all kinds of historical details. Dickens stated his historical intentions in his preface to *Barnaby Rudge:* "No account of the Gordon Riots having been to my knowledge introduced into any Work . . . and the subject presenting very extraordinary and remarkable features, I was led to project this Tale." (Not only did *Barnaby Rudge* turn out to be a good tale; it also preceded the first historical monograph of the Gordon Riots [1780] by more than a century.)

Second: the novelist's description of contemporary scenes which he himself witnessed is often first-rate historical evidence. "Fiction is often an aid to history," Alfred Duff Cooper wrote, "and the penetrating eye of genius can discern much that remains elusive to the patient researches of the historian." I have often thought that Stendhal's (rather than Hugo's) description of Waterloo in *The Charterhouse of Parma* ought to be required reading in our military colleges, since it is such a telling corrective to abstract schemes of battle orders — as well as to the false image of nineteenth-century battles as long *mêlées* among brightly uniformed soldiers, punctuated by flashes of bayonets, the sabers of cavalry charging, and the Beethovenian sound of cannon in the background, always booming in C major. Maupassant's brillant short story "Coup d'état" ought to be printed in our dreary readers in political science because of its superb description of how unrevolutionary certain revolutions have been, since it is such a corrective to such clichés as "the people rose against the established order," etc. On the level of social and intellectual history a novel such as *New Grub Street* not only is full of historical evidences about London in the 1880s, about how some people lived, and about the conditions of the literary industry at that time; it also reveals a whole category of late-Victorian sensibilities.

Third: the novelists' description of certain fictitious characters may serve the historian on occasion: when, for example, these are prototypical representatives of their classes and times. Trollope's Duke of Omnium, Flaubert's Emma Bovary, Arnold Bennett's Constance Baines, Sinclair Lewis's George Babbitt are renditions of potential historical characters. I am not contrasting "the real flesh and blood" characters of a novelist with the "paper and paste" figures of a professor. I am arguing that the existence of a type of, say, Monsieur Homais belongs to the history of nineteenth-century France, and that an understanding of the particular circumstances of Emma Bovary's problems and tragedy should be a requirement for those who wish to understand her "times," being something more than a novelist's evocative limning of an "atmosphere." Fictional characters may represent tendencies, about the existence of which actual historical evidence is available elsewhere. Even a deliberate exaggeration, a satire, may be a guide to historical understanding; a sensitive historian may use it for sake of illustration. On page 139 of his excellent history of the summer of 1940, *Operation Sea Lion,* Peter Fleming cites an actual asininity, a bureaucrat's statement at the time, to which then he adds this judicious footnote: "For a satirical pastiche — from which the above sentence might well be taken — purporting to describe the religious activities of the Ministry of Information in 1940 see *Put Out More Flags* by Evelyn Waugh (London, 1942). This novel is an excellent guide to the atmosphere of the period."

If certain statistics are historical documents, so are certain characters composed by novelists out of their imagination as well as out of reality — of historical imagination and historical reality.

Finally, in the fourth place, literary history belongs within history, not merely as its cultural appendix, as Trevelyan once put it, "like the tail of a cow." On the one hand great literature has had an enduring influence — though sometimes only in the long run. On the other hand evidences of the short run, too, may be significant: the very history of books, including novels, the circumstances of their publications, their critical or popular success, and sometimes their rejection too. A novel may articulate, generate, speed up, slow down currents of opinion, social and cultural tendencies. Sometimes these relationships are traceable: *Werther* or Scott come to mind; and in 1951 the fine Indian writer and scholar Nirad C. Chaudhuri wrote that

reading *A Passage to India* some time ago I was led to think not only of the final collective passage of the British from India but also of Mr. Forster's contribution to that finale. Such an association of ideas between a novel and an event of political history may be objected to, but in this case I think the association is legitimate. For *A Passage to India* has possibly been an even greater influence in British imperial politics than in English literature. . . . The novel helped the growth of that mood which enabled the British people to leave India with an almost Pilate-like gesture of washing their hands of a disagreeable affair.

All of this may be rather obvious. But let us now look at the other side of the relationship: at the historicity of the novel.

The novel grew with history. The modern novel began to appear after 1750, professional history after 1777; by 1780 there were best-seller novels. After 1800 there came another variant: the historical novel, in which history is the colorful and often dramatic background, to make the story and its actors seem especially interesting. Thereafter the nineteenth century was the golden age of the novel. It was then impregnated with the consciousness of history. Not only are *Old Mortality, Les Chouans, A Tale of Two Cities, The Charterhouse of Parma, War and Peace* historical novels; so are *César Birotteau, Martin Chuzzlewit, Lucien Leuwen, Sentimental Education.* Let me pause here for a moment. Let me argue that Flaubert's *Sentimental Education* is *more historical* than its near-contemporary *War and Peace,* even though the latter is generally classified as a "historical" novel while the former is not. For the "history" in *War and Peace,* no matter how dramatic and explicit, is often incorrect and superficial, whereas the history in *Sentimental Education* is implicit and often deep-going. Flaubert's portrait of 1848 is, historically speaking, more complex and more meaningful than Tolstoy's of 1812, because Flaubert describes how people thought and felt at that time; his novel abounds with descriptions of changing sensitivities, of mutations of opinions and transformations of attitudes. In spite (or, perhaps, because) of Tolstoy's decision for writing a "scientific" history, *War and Peace* reflects a kind of ideological, rather than historical, thinking. Flaubert, without knowing it,* was the more historical writer of the two, perhaps because of how historical thinking had penetrated the Western mind by 1850. Thereafter more and more novels became historical sociographies, a development reaching its peak around 1900. Arnold Bennett was not a greater writer than Laurence Sterne, Thomas Mann than Goethe, Roger Martin du Gard than Victor Hugo; but the former's novels are soaked with history. *The Old Wives' Tale, Buddenbrooks, Les Thibault* are grand bourgeois novels, more "deeply" historical than some of their forerunners.

The history of American prose literature is somewhat dif-

---

* His attempt at an epic "historical" novel of antiquity, *Salammbô,* was a failure.

ferent. Poe's and Melville's novels are something else than the European (and even English) historical novels. Even *Washington Square* and *The Age of Innocence* are predominantly sociographic, even more than historical. Yet *The Great Gatsby* is, among its other virtues, historical — while its contemporary, Dreiser's *An American Tragedy*, is not.*

4.

Every novel is a historical novel, in one way or another. To recognize this is as important for a historian as it is for a novelist. "Readers of Alexandre Dumas may be potential historians," wrote the great French historian Marc Bloch. Maupassant wrote in his only essay, disguised as his preface to *Pierre et Jean*, that the aim of the realistic novelist "is not to tell a story, to amuse us or to appeal to our feelings, but *to compel us to reflect, and to understand the darker and deeper meaning of events*" (italics mine). A thoughtful historian should understand this, as it goes beyond (and beneath) the, now probably antiquated, genre of the classic "historical novel."

To prove that every novel is a historical novel consider now Jane Austen's preface (she called it "Advertisement by the Authoress") to her *Northanger Abbey*, in 1816:

* See my essay *"The Great Gatsby? Yes, a Historical Novel,"* in *Novel History: Historians and Novelists Confront America's Past (and Each Other)*, ed. Mark C. Carnes (New York, 2001).

This little work was finished in the year 1803, and intended for immediate publication. It was disposed of to a bookseller, it was even advertised, and why the business proceeded no farther, the author has never been able to learn. That any bookseller should think it worth-while to purchase what he did not think it worth-while to publish seems extraordinary. But with this, neither the author nor the public have any other concern *than as some observation is necessary upon those parts of the work which thirteen years have made comparatively obsolete. The public are entreated to bear in mind that thirteen years have passed since it was finished, many more since it was begun, and that during that period, places, manners, books, and opinions have undergone considerable changes.*

My italicized passages should make it unnecessary to press the point: within her storytelling, Jane Austen's concern was decidedly and evidently historical.

Eighty years later Thomas Hardy wrote:

Conscientious fiction alone it is which can excite a reflecting and abiding interest in the minds of thoughtful readers of mature age, who are weary of puerile inventions and famishing for accuracy; who consider that in representations of the world the passions ought to be proportioned as in the world itself.

This is the interest which was excited in the minds of Athenians by their immortal tragedies, and in the minds of Londoners at the first performance of the finer plays of three hundred years ago.*

Another 120 years later it is my conviction that conscientious history may be replacing that desideratum that Hardy stated as conscientious fiction. It is history which can excite a reflecting and abiding interest in the minds of thoughtful readers of mature age, who are weary (and how weary we are!) of puerile inventions and are famishing for accuracy — I should add: for truthfulness.

5.

There is a difference between importance and significance, between "important" and "significant" events. The meaning of the latter is that their effect is less immediate and decisive than potential, like the appearance of a small crack on a large solid surface.†

The eyes of novelists have been especially attracted to significant matters (acts, words, even gestures, even si-

* Hardy, "Candour in English Fiction," cited in J. Korg, *George Gissing: A Critical Biography* (Seattle, 1979), 261.
† Often I have been charmed by the frequent use of "signify" in Victorian English: "It does not signify," or "that would not signify." Meaning: it is not important (at least not now).

lences) within their stories. They were significant: because of their potentiality. But a historian, too, must consider — or at least keep in mind — the unavoidable existence of potentialities. There is here a corresponding epistemological discovery in quantum physics, since in subatomic physics physicists are observing not only *actual* but also potential events. And here I must, with bated breath, think beyond Aristotle. "The poet and the historian," he said in *Poetics* (IX, 17), "differ not by writing in verse or prose. The work of Herodotus might be put in verse and it still would be a species of history with meter no less than without it. The true difference is that one relates what happened, the other what may happen. Poetry, therefore, is a more philosophic and higher thing than history, for poetry *tends* to express the universal, history the particular." (By italicizing "tends" *I* try to suggest that perhaps not even Aristotle made the categories absolute.)

Midway between poetry and history, then, the classical novel tended to express not quite *what has happened,* not quite *what may happen,* but, rather, *what might have happened.* Earlier (and perhaps throughout this book) I have insisted that people do not "have" ideas but that they choose them. To this I now add that while it may be important what ideas do to men, it is often even more important what people do with their ideas. What people do and did, yes: but also what they were capable of doing, and thinking.

The modern historian, too, cannot exclude the contemplation of possibilities. (The — relative — success of my *The Duel* and *Five Days in London,* dealing with May–July 1940, was largely due to the re-cognition by their readers of how close Hitler had come to winning the war then. For the motto of *The Duel* I chose a passage by Huizinga, who wrote that the historian, writing of the battle of Salamis [480 B.C.], must keep in mind that the Persians could "still win.") While potentialities alone, without their actual expressions, cannot constitute historical evidence (this being one of the few correspondences between historical and legal evidence, at least in the Western world), the purposes of history and of law are different. The purpose of law is to maintain justice by eliminating injustice; the purpose of history is to pursue truth by eliminating untruths. And the historian's recognition that reality encompasses actuality and potentiality reflects his propensity to see things with the eye of a novelist rather than with the eye of a lawyer.

6.

In the second half of the eighteenth century the novel and professional historianship came at the same time. Now their crisis appears at the same time too, in the second half of the twentieth century.

Reasons for the crisis of the novel are of course related to contemporary history, to changes in the structure of societies and in that of certain events. To begin with: Fact has often become stranger than Fiction. (I am not mentioning the juvenile genre of science fiction.) There are matters such as life in Auschwitz, or two men walking on the moon, subjects about which a novel would make not much sense, subjects less human than what a novelist would imagine. I am also thinking of the maddening nonsense that rises around us every day and night, evident in all kinds of advertisements, slogans, publicity promotions, technological and puerile lingo, the sounds and screams of popular music, etc. This kind of stuff can hardly be parodied or satirized, since it consists less of distortions of realities than of exaggerations of already existing senselessness. The necessary imagination of the novelist falters not only in face of monstrosities but also in face of the deadening accumulation of nonsense in this age of universal literacy when we encounter such banalities in conversations, such mistakes in public rhetoric, that their very accurate recording would result in an impression of unreal exaggerations.*

One, probably even more important, reason for the

---

* Herbert Butterfield sixty or so years ago: "The historian, like the novelist, is bound to be glad that it takes all sorts of men to make a world. Like the novelist he can regret only one kind — the complete bore — and take care not to describe him with too great verisimilitude."

crisis of the novel is the in places almost complete disappearance of classes. For the standard subjects of the novel involved always, in some way or another, the relationships of the inner lives of persons with the external structure of society. But large portions of this scaffolding of society have now been dismantled or have simply disappeared, a development corresponding to the relative formlessness of the democratic texture of history. Social relationships, social ambitions, social aspirations have become widely meaningless. (A few great novelists had seen this coming. Thus more than one hundred years ago the Spanish Galdós: "The confusion of classes is the counterfeit coin of equality." One hundred years later our contemporary V. S. Naipaul: "A literature can grow only out of a strong framework of social conventions.")

This dissolution of classes, society, etc., led many a novelist in the twentieth century to contemplate increasingly an individual's relationship with himself. This awareness of self-consciousness reflects the crisis of the novel, as it involves the consciousness of the narrator. Thus the collapse of the once dominant ideal of complete objectivity has affected the novelist as he became aware of the impossibility (and artificiality) of the impartial, detached stance from which an invisible narrator, equipped with an Olympian eye, told what third persons did and thought and felt. So novelists resorted to all kinds of devices: establishing the narrator in the first person singular;* at times inside the brain and the nervous ganglia of the protagonist or antihero; inventing a storyteller within a storyteller; and, in the end, novels about novels. We must also understand why the stream-of-consciousness method of re-creating deeper human realities is necessarily incomplete: because people do not necessarily *think* in the way they *speak*. Whence Joyce's *Ulysses* (as also Céline's monologues) are period pieces, dated. Many such experiments have led to a dead end.

The novel has been affected by the cultural and civilizational crisis of the twentieth century even more than has historiography. Whereas in the nineteenth century the novel was a narrative and descriptive form of art, in the twentieth century this once standard endeavor began to dissolve, in two directions. The first tendency moves toward poetry, the other toward history. Of course there was always poetry in passages of great prose. There are memorable poetic phrases and passages that have come down to us, that we remember not from poems but from novels.

---

* I found an interesting "solution" in Jean Dutourd's *Les Horreurs de l'amour* ("The horrors of love," 1963), written, it may be said, in the second person singular: the relationships of third persons are reconstructed through a running conversation between two friends (a technique — or, rather, an approach — which could, I believe, be applied to the unraveling of certain historical problems by an audacious historian someday).

(The "green light" at the end of *The Great Gatsby,* etc., etc.) Many of the recent experiments of absurd, comic, involuted, "new" novels amount to attempts at grappling with poetic language. Few of them will endure, despite their "internalization." Yet one day a "new" novelist may succeed in breaking through to a new genre — but perhaps only on the condition that he is something else than a habitual novelist, that he be able to produce a new form of meaningful lyrical narration.

The other tendency leads, more and more, toward history, toward writing history of some kind. Of course professional, scientific, objective historiography, typical of the spirit of the bourgeois age, no more exhausted the function of history than the nineteenth-century novel exhausted the function of of prose literature. Yet I believe that the demise of the historical novel has been followed by the novel's absorption by history. Talented men who in the nineteenth century were attracted to novel writing turned later to history writing. One hundred fifty years ago Disraeli wrote novels; one hundred years ago Churchill wrote histories. Another fifty years later we can see the growth of popular interest in good history rather than in good fiction, the appetite of people for historical reconstructions. This new phenomenon is there in many things, among them the decline of interest in flamboyant "historical" novels, and the rise of interest in the "documentary" genre. The latter, with all of its shortcomings, represents something more than a journalistic technique. The "documentary" is but one manifestation of the unfolding of the representation of history in many ways. It is an attempt at reconstructing some portion of a particular kind of reality too in a historical past.

It has now appeared in many countries, on television, films, etc. Historians must take it, with all of its variations, into account. So must the remaining novelists. To say, as Truman Capote said, that the historical reconstruction he had attempted in a recent book (*In Cold Blood,* 1964) amounts to a new kind of novel, "the nonfiction novel," is shallow; it is not enough. We are witnessing the reformation of the novel by poetry on the one hand, its conquest by history on the other. In the old historical novel human figures were the protagonists; history provided the background. Then, increasingly, history has become the protagonist, the foreground. Three hundred years ago, as he set out on his *Age of Louis XIV,* Voltaire wrote: "The principal figures are in the foreground, the crowd is in the background. Woe to details! Posterity neglects them all; they are a kind of vermin that undermines large works." But now the opposite: the Historical Background becoming The Foreground. In a "documentary" historical novel the entire plot is History; the characters are secondary, here and there representing political or other opinions; while their portraiture is overwhelmed by History.

There is a danger here. When people are thus overwhelmed by "the march of history," this suggests that their freedom of will is hopelessly curtailed, that their aspirations are bereft of much meaning, that they are supernumeraries. The result is the confusion of what is only imaginary with what was historically real, instead of a proper comprehension of their complementarity: imaginary matters (and often imaginary people) are introduced, illegitimately, into "history." There exist now "historical" novels where once living, actual persons are made to appear and act and talk fictitiously for the purposes of the novelist author. (For example: J. P. Morgan in Doctorow's *Ragtime;* or Charles Lindbergh in Philip Roth's *The Plot Against America.* There are many more instances of this.) In these novels History *is* the foreground, but it is a twisted and false history.

For, even when it comes to potentialities, the historian, like the novelist, may describe what might have happened (and not only what happened): but only on the basis of actual evidence. And while the novelist, by creating his characters, may attribute motives to them — indeed his description of their intentions may be even more important than the description of their actions — the historian must proceed on the basis of the primacy of actual expressions and actions. The novelist must of course make the connection between motives and actions plausible: but he does not sin by inventing motives for his characters. The historian does. About this too the historian's task is the more difficult one.

7.

There has now appeared a new kind of literature that is essentially and consciously history-minded. I wrote that, especially during the second half of the twentieth century, the novel was tending in two directions: one toward poetry, the other toward history. Of the two, the tendency toward history has been the stronger, the more evident. The cultural crisis affected poetry worse than it affected history.* Meanwhile the novelists' attraction toward history has become more and more evident. At least during the past fifty years they have been mixing fact and fiction — a few call this "faction," a silly word — building on and

* The great Hungarian Catholic poet János Pilinszky, circa 1980: "The novel is the only real genre (perhaps the drama, too, but only to an extent) the subject of which is *time*. No other form of art can deal with that, and yet it is the driving force of the novel. And therefore I regret when the novel in the twentieth century begins to move toward poetry." (Note that this was written by a poet.) The Swiss Max Picard, 1946: "Poetry no longer makes silence sound."

around chunks of history. But this mixture in their novels has often been imprecise, illegitimate, indiscriminating, manipulative — as in so many movies.

Here is a — very random — sample list of this "new" kind of novel, from about 1920 to 1990: *Tsushima* by Frank Thiess (one of the first and perhaps the best of the lot), *Stalingrad* and *Moskau* by Theodor Plievier, *Lanny Budd* by Upton Sinclair, *Men of Good Will* by Jules Romains, *Nineteen-Nineteen* by John Dos Passos, *The Winds of War* by Herman Wouk, *The Fox in the Attic* by Richard Hughes, *In Cold Blood* by Truman Capote, *Ragtime* by E. L. Doctorow, *History: A Novel* by Elsa Morante. (This title is telling. Her book is very bad.) Now add to this — I repeat, very incomplete — list such books confected during the past thirty years, perhaps 1980 to 2010, by Irwin Shaw, Susan Sontag, Gore Vidal, Thomas Pynchon, Philip Roth,* Nor-

---

* Roth's case is very telling. The work of this talented Jewish American writer progressed from *Goodbye Columbus,* a melancholy novel involving the relationship and conflicts of a young man and a young woman of different classes, to other novels describing mostly the complicated and uneasy aspirations of Jewish Americans at considerable depths — always aware of the manners and mores of their times — to *The Plot Against America,* an imaginary political history of 1940–43, of a nation where Charles Lindbergh, the sympathizer of Germany and Hitler, succeeds Franklin Roosevelt as president. A very bad book, chock full of historical mistakes and misrepresentations. (Seventy years before Roth, Sinclair Lewis wrote *It Can't Happen Here,* 1935, the theme of this novel being life during a populist right-wing dictatorship that *could* happen in the United States, but a book largely devoid of history. The

man Mailer (whose last book would have been a "faction" about the young Adolf Hitler. Mailer's death then spared him and his readers from much embarrassment) — and many others abroad, including Solzhenitsyn's *1914* (which is his least valuable book).

So — all of these novelists have been interested in history, perhaps even before everything else. But have they understood that they were writing the very opposites of the historical novel, where history was the background and not the foreground? Did any of them consciously attempt to construct, or to break through to, a new genre? Plainly: did they know what they were doing? It does not seem so. Perhaps this is why so many of these books are flawed, when they include and twist and deform and attribute thoughts and words and acts to men and women (James Buchanan, Morgan, Wilson, Roosevelt, Lindbergh, etc.) who actually existed. That is wrong, because it produces untruths — no matter how some historians say that it serves salutary purposes, since it introduces all kinds of people to history after all. Yet wrong or right — more is involved here than "faction."*

---

theme of Philip Roth's book, suffused with history, is that *it could have happened here*.)

* While writing this book I read a recent novel by the estimable British writer A. S. Byatt (*The Children's Book*), describing the growing up and then the lives of one generation, approximately from 1890 to 1920. She felt compelled to add to her chapters long summaries of the politi-

Now consider, for the last time, Tolstoy. The history in *War and Peace* is falsified and distorted by Tolstoy's opinions and prejudices, not only about Napoleon and his wars but about history itself. In the long appendix that Tolstoy felt compelled to add to his massive novel he propounded an antihistorical philosophy of history that is utter nonsense. Tolstoy the novelist is not separable from Tolstoy the philosopher of history (which is what Isaiah Berlin did in his clever essay "The Hedgehog and the Fox"), since many of the weird ideas of that appendix appear earlier, too, within the narrative novel itself. Ninety years after *War and Peace* Boris Pasternak's *Doctor Zhivago* was not suffused with a philosophy of history. It was not a historical drama like *War and Peace*. Yet Pasternak's reconstruction of what happened in Russia, and in some Russian minds, and to certain Russian people from 1917 to 1924, is more historical than Tolstoy's rendition of history between 1805 and 1812. And when we look at the task assumed by Aleksandr Solzhenitsyn, we can see his main purpose: to set history right; to reduce untruth. (In *The Gulag Archipelago:* "We forget everything. What we remember is not what actually happened, not history, but merely that hackneyed dotted line they have chosen to

---

cal, etc., history of a particular year or period. Why? To give more substance to her story? Probably so. (At least I know no novelist who attempted something like this method before.)

drive into our memories by incessant hammering." From *Ivan Denisovich* through *The Gulag Archipelago* to *August 1914* and *Lenin in Zurich,* Solzhenitsyn's interest has been increasingly historical. The meaning of this evolution may be obscured by some of Solzhenitsyn's ideological pronouncements and the Slavophile excrescences of his thinking: still, his addiction to history is a symptom of the development of historical consciousness in the twentieth century — while Tolstoy's genre of the historical novel belongs to a receding and antiquated past.

These examples of Pasternak and Solzhenitsyn include, of course, particular responses in a country long burdened by oppressive conditions. But the issue of a spreading historical consciousness is larger than that. It may even be possible that in the future the novel may be entirely absorbed by history. We must not speculate about this further. But that history — in one form or another — will survive the novel we ought to know.

A small addendum

The relationship (and at times the concordance) of history and the novel interested me since my early youth. I wrote (and spoke) about this relationship in articles, and at some length in *Historical Consciousness* and in its subsequent editions (1968, 1985, 1994), so much so that in this present chapter I drew upon a few such paragraphs, paraphrasing or summing them up. Here in *The Future of History* I have suggested that something of a new kind of history might appear, though not predicting how and what this may be. But in the 1990s something compelled me to try my hand at it—except that it was not *it* but something quite different. The result was my *A Thread of Years,* published in 1998 by Yale University Press, which I still (2011) consider as my most extraordinary book.

I set out my reasons for it in an introduction (contrary to my inclination that good books need little or no introductions, they ought to speak for themselves). But *A Thread of Years* was, and is, different. I did the opposite from what the writers mentioned in the foregoing pages were doing. Instead of attributing acts, words, thoughts to famous people who did exist, I described imaginary people whose plausibility existed only because of the historical realities of their places and their times. *A Thread of Years* consists of sixty-nine chapters or chapterettes, each with the title of a year: "1901" (the first), or "1914," or "1969" (the last). These chapterettes consist of two parts. The first part is a vignette, about episodes in the lives of various people, in Philadelphia or Paris or London or elsewhere, in 1901 or 1911 or 1925, etc., etc. Vignettes describing *them* but within a vague or vast and potentially significant, sometimes ominous or threatening, sometimes pleasing but evanescent historical atmosphere.

Thus, for example, the end of July in "1914," in Paris, is not about the coming of the war, though some of that atmosphere suffuses the vignette: it is about men and women in a particular place at a particular time, how they behaved and looked, how they spoke and thought and felt and believed. The second part of each chapterette is my dialogue with an imaginary conversant (yes, he is one side of myself) who challenges either the historicity or the accuracy of the vignette, attempting to reduce what may be imprecise or not quite plausible in it. So someone may say that the first part of each chapterette (the vignette — often something like an unfinished short story) — is by a novelist, the second by a historian. *Not* really. *All* of this book is the production of a historian, such as myself.

Now for historians: let me tell them right away and now: *A Thread of Years* is *not* a new kind of history (even though this is what a few of its sympathetic reviewers wrote). Almost all of the men and women therein are imagined: this excludes them from history. What are not imagined are the places and the times of the vignettes. They *are* history all right; perhaps — I hope — some of them even better than all right. Often I have wished that someone would adopt my method and try his hand at something similar (Yes: to do that he ought to know much history). But *A Thread of Years* is neither a history nor a novel.

SIX

Future of the Profession

Future of books and of reading ♦ History is necessarily revisionist ♦ Pursuit of justice; pursuit of truth ♦ Shortsightedness
of American liberal historians. Ideas and beliefs

I.

Until now I wrote much — perhaps too much — about the
state of history at the present time (2011). In some ways
optimistically: that "history" has a future; that there is a
new and widespread appetite for history; that much good
history is written and published even now; that history
may even absorb the novel. Some of these developments
may go on and on. But I cannot be optimistic about the
future.

We cannot know much about the future, save project-
ing what we can see at present: but so much of that will
not come about. Some of it will. Foresight is something
else than prophecy: foresight depends on a serious, some-

times inspired knowledge and understanding of some things in the past. Through this some of us may know that this or that will not happen; but also that this or that, lo and behold, might. The movements of history are not mechanical, not clocklike, not pendular. Reaching an extreme arc the pendulum moves back, but in another direction.

So, at least so I think, there will be no reversal. The teaching of history in our schools may decrease further. Fewer intelligent young students will opt for a career requiring a doctorate in history. We already know that fewer and fewer among our best students read. What vexes my mind even more: will the still present interest in history books and biographies continue? Will this, relatively new and recent, appetite for history prevail? Much of that depends on publishers and on other — not always inspired — promoters. There are plenty of examples in the democratic age when fairly widespread and exceptional tendencies faded and then disappeared, because they were no longer promoted by publicity. At this time publishers still know that histories outsell novels; but does this mean that they are inspired by that condition? It does not seem so. Their dependence on quick, indeed instant, profits began at least fifty years ago; the same applies to television or movie producers. The structure of events, including the movements of people's mental interests, is now complicated enough for us to identify the managed influence of publicity within them. In this, as in many other things, the term "consumer society" may be misleading, since the consumption of production depends on the — much more complicated — production of consumption, actual and potential. (Thus, for example, the diminution and the disappearance of newspapers reduces not only the availability of information but the habits and custom of reading.)

For many serious professional historians their opportunities and conditions of publication are shrinking at an alarming rate. A normal print-run (first printing) at many, if not most, university presses is now five hundred or even fewer (mostly because the number of college and university libraries customarily purchasing such titles has decreased by fifty percent or more). As a consequence, many serious monographs and even other works of professional historical scholarship have become excessively expensive; worse — they may not even appear on the shelves of bookstores, including the once inclusive university bookstores. The results of this devolution are frightening. (Surely they must frighten young aspiring historians within the profession.)

Will the current difference between "professional" and "amateur" historians narrow or widen? I cannot tell. The main subject of this book, and perhaps especially this chapter, is directed to the actual and potential problems of professionals: yet one more rumination may be in order here about "amateur," that is, nonacademic, writers of history. Their motives, their genuine interest in history will not, I think, disappear, and probably not much diminish either. I even find it possible that the best (by this I mean much more than the most readable) histories in the near future may be written by nonacademics. But—I am now peering with my old tired eyes toward a darkening future —what will happen with their purposes when the world of books disappears? The purpose of a writer is, after all, to see his book published, and then hope that people, many kinds of people, may read it. (This purpose of "amateur" historians is clearer than is the case of at least some academic historians when the purpose of their completion of their book involves, besides publication, their academic advancement.) Isn't the writing of history, at least as we know it, bound to books? Allow me to attempt speculating about this in the next, and last, chapter of this little book.

But now back to professionals. What are their principal tasks and responsibilities during this large transition that is already upon us, from a verbal to a pictorial era, toward a new kind of barbarism,* replete with new dangers?

* Recall that the original meaning of "civilization" (*O.E.D.:* 1,601) was "the emergence from barbarism."

2.

One of the many differences between the achievements of historical and the applications of "scientific" knowledge is that the former is necessarily "revisionist." Professional historians must recognize this. Among some of them the older nineteenth-century view, according to which the Cathedral of History is being built brick upon brick by certified professional historians, still prevails. But there is no such cathedral, because the building of it, or even portions of it, can never be completed. Yes, there are gaps of historical knowledge that are, or ought to be, filled: but that filling can never be permanent. We have seen that near the end of the nineteenth century Acton said that a historical account of the Battle of Waterloo may now be constructed that would be acceptable to British and French and German and Dutch historians. He expected too much of scientific objectivity: even more, he believed that such an account would be *definite* and *final*. But all history is revisionist, in one way or another.

In the Compact Edition of the *Oxford English Dictionary* the word "revisionism" does not appear. Revision, says the *O.E.D.,* is "the action of revising or looking over again, esp. critical or careful examination or perusal with a view of correcting or improving." The related entries do not mention historians.* ("Revisionists" in Britain in the 1880s were clergymen working on revising portions of the Bible.) Perhaps the first, and most eminent, example of a writer whose main purpose was to revise and correct and, when necessary, eliminate then current versions of legends and mistakes was Thucydides, as he stated in his introduction to the *History of the Peloponnesian War.* That historians and chroniclers had on occasion questioned or corrected versions of legends is of course obvious. But there were not many instances when the works of chroniclers were mostly aimed at disproving other chroniclers' versions. After 1700 in France there appeared a group of scholarly priests (especially Mabillon and Tillemont) who, for the first time, applied critical methods to their examination of medieval texts and of questionable legends and sources. These so-called Erudites or Antiquaries were perhaps the first modern and specialist historians. Yet soon their reputation faded. Instead, the professional study of history and the establishing of professional historianship arose in Germany, spreading thereafter across Europe. Then for about a century the aim of professional historians was a magisterial filling of large gaps, including necessary revisions of dubious accounts. Criticisms of the accepted versions

* Wendell Berry in a letter to this author (9 February 2010: "Our 'reality' is constantly in need of revision—which is maybe the best argument for freedom of thought and speech."

of events established by professional historians were relatively rare.

Then another particular use of "revisionism" came out of Germany after the First World War.* Its aim was to correct the inaccurate and unilateral condemnation of Germany as having been primarily responsible for the outbreak of World War I, as also stated in the Treaty of Versailles. The Germans had every reason to combat that. As early as in 1919 the new republican German government began to publish documents to prove that the responsibility for the outbreak of the war in 1914 was not Germany's alone. More extensive documentation was then published in a series of volumes. In 1923 a German amateur historian, Alfred von Wegerer, started issuing a scholarly journal, *Die Kriegsschuldfrage,* The War Guilt Question. By that time, and then especially thereafter, certain American professional historians (as well as some amateurs) were writing books supporting the German cause.

*The term "revisionism" was first applied to those German Socialists who, around 1875, chose to reduce the doctrine of the inevitability of a proletarian revolution. This Marxist usage does not concern us. But there is an entry for "revisionism" in the 1987 *Supplement* of the *O.E.D.,* where, among other subheadings, "historical revisionism" appears: "a movement to rewrite the accepted version of American history, esp. those relating to foreign affairs, since the war of 1939–1945." This is incorrect, because the first widespread "revisionism" among American historians involved the interpretation of the First, not of the Second, World War, in many books and articles.

A few years later other serious books appeared, revising and dismissing the entire accepted version of the circumstances and purposes of America's entry into World War I in 1917.

There was, and there remains, sufficient substance in some of these books for us to peruse some of their evidences even now. Yet there are at least two reasons why we ought to consider their, eventually deleterious, consequences. One involves the time lag in the movements of ideas. Books and articles radically revising the accepted ideas about World War I in the United States began to trickle down to the reading public as well as to many historians about ten years after 1917. Another ten years later these revisionist interpretations had reached a popular level, often asserted by national political figures. The result was that "isolationist" (or "noninterventionist" or "pacifist" — none of these designations is accurate but that is not the point here) sentiments among the American people reached their peak around 1937, when the power of Hitler's Germany was rising. It took Pearl Harbor, almost five years later, to decisively weaken the appeal of American isolationist sentiments and opinions — which in the meantime had been the main obstacles to President Roosevelt's world policy even when Hitler was conquering most of Europe and threatening to extirpate Britain.

The other lamentable consequence was that many

(though not all) of the chief American revisionist historians of the 1920s, often smarting from the criticisms of
their opponents and fired up with anger, went on attack-
ing American "interventionism" and Roosevelt's support
of Britain and China (and then of Russia) during — and
well after — the Second World War, thus directly or indi-
rectly supporting the causes of Germany (and sometimes
even of Japan). Their books and articles published after
the war were less popular than revisionism had been after
World War I in the 1920s, though we must not underesti-
mate their appeal even now. (Among other matters, their
readers and believers were one substantial core group of
the rising American "conservative" movement in 1950 and
after, about which in this chapter anon.)

There were, and are, and will be, many kinds of revisionism. Some of their potential attractions and actual
followers are ideological. They may be the bane of historians, and not only of those who might be mesmerized by
certain documents. This does not mean a defense of "or-
thodox" history because there is no such thing. But the
revising of history must not be an ephemeral monopoly of
ideologues or opportunists who are ever ready to twist or
even falsify documentary evidences of the past in order to
exemplify current ideas — and their own adjustments to
them.

Such dangers are now greater (and probably more frequent) than before. The forgery and the falsification of documents have now become more feasible technically than before. (A new and insidious practice is not the filching of documents from archives but the insertion of false documents into archival files, an easy practice against which archivists have little or no protection.) More than once I have experienced significant forgeries created by very knowledgeable individuals about people and events of World War II. And here the tasks and responsibilities of professional historians must enter. It is they, working in and knowing their genuine interests, who must find and point out the falseness of this or that document (and of its interpretation). This calls for serious archival knowledge and practice — and a willingness to face the prospect that their revelation may go unnoticed save for a few professionals with some specialized interest in such a subject. And, beneath and above all this, a dedication to truth finding within their craft.

It is regrettable that some leading and reputable historians miss this. One example: their customary dismissal of the obsessed "revisionist" David Irving because of his ideology, while admitting that Irving's archival researches are considerable. Yet when I, in one instance, felt compelled to find and look up one of Irving's footnotes with its detailed microfilm references, I found (I admit: with some relief) that the document which he had cited to sustain his argument was entirely irrelevant to it.

3.

The authentic quality of sources and evidences for historians has now become more complicated than before, because (rather than despite) their multiplicity. There *is* an essential difference not only between historical and "scientific" but also between historical and legal evidences — and, even more important, between their very purposes. The law has its rules. It is an institutionalized system. In civilized states law does not allow multiple jeopardy: an accused person may be tried only once. But history consists of an endless reconsideration of men and events in the past — moreover: evidences not only of their acts but also of their thoughts, evidences thus admissible in history but not in law. The administration of laws, in civilized states, may not admit potentialities. (Samuel Johnson: "Intentions must be gathered from acts.") Law will admit a "motive" but only if and when it has been evidently expressed, in one way or another: in other words, an actuality. (A unique characteristic of Western Christianity, too, is that it says little or nothing about motives of evil [save for the recognition of the original sin of mankind], while it says plenty about its evidences, not only in acts but also in speech and thought.)

"The law is a coarse net; and truth is a slippery fish." Yes: but a net, however coarse, is better than no net at all. Yet the purpose of law has little (and sometimes nothing) to do with truth. It is the establishment of justice — or, more precisely, the protection against injustice. And justice is of a lower order than is truth (and untruth is lower than injustice. All of Christ's parables taught people to follow truth, not justice). The administration of justice, even with the best of intentions for correcting injustice, may often have to overlook or even ignore untruths during the judicial process. People live and are capable of living with injustices; but a worse shortcoming is their self-willed choice to live with untruths. No need to argue this further here, except to recognize that the differences between the propagations of justice and the prevalences of untruths are extensive now, at the end of the so-called Modern Age. The governments of many states and all kinds of legal institutions profess to dedicate themselves to the reduction of injustices: against slavery, exploitations, racial and sexual discriminations, etc. Yet few people are aware that an indiscriminate pursuit of justice may be carried to insane lengths — that, indeed, it may lay much of the world to waste. (Consider some of the atrocious techniques of recent wars; or of the American and puritanical character and fate of Captain Ahab in *Moby-Dick.*)

But then the purpose of history, too, is less a definite establishment of truths than it is the reduction of untruths. Nearly four hundred years ago Descartes, in his *Discourse on Method,* argued, or at least suggested, that the study of history was wasteful, because we cannot acquire any accurate or certain knowledge of the human past, as we can of mathematics and of the world of nature. Less than a century after Descartes, Vico said the opposite. The world of men, "the civil world," was a reality, not an invention — to which let me add that while the natural world and the universe exist, our knowledge of their existence is not independent from ourselves and from our ever changing perceptions and inventions of them: another argument, and evidence, of the inseparability of the knower from the known.

The historian, at best, ought to do better than did Pontius Pilate (whom I, for one, could never contemplate without at least a modicum of sympathy). But when Pilate asked: "What is truth?" he also implied: "What is untruth?" The historian ought to see untruth when it appears. His work consists of the pursuit of truth (where Pilate had stopped), often hacking his way through jungles of untruths, trees, saplings, bushes, shrubs, and many, many weeds, large and small ones.

4.

At least a quarter of a century has now passed since historians began to use computers. When, more than a century ago, they had begun to type on typewriters, that did not change the composition, the style, the practices or the subjects of their researches and of their writing. When it came to computers this may or may not be so. Entire books have now been written about the relationships of human intelligence and computers. I know nothing about that topic; but, concerned with the present and the future of historianship, allow me to suggest two observations.

One is that, whether in writing history or other kinds of literature, there is no evidence that composing on a computer improves the writer's style — in some cases, rather the contrary. The other, and larger, problem consists in the reliance of a researcher on the information available to him on a computer. The quantities of that kind of "information" are of course very large and astonishingly convenient. But are they reliable? Yes and no. They have been "programmed," that is, put into the computer by anonymous machines and men and women. There are entire "data banks" where important things, including the very existence of certain books or articles or other materials, are absent — and will continue being absent. Of this many (if not most) people using computers are ignorant (consider only students relying on texts or quotes or references from computers for stuffing these into their papers). "Retrievable" and "reliable" are not the same things; and what, after having pressed some buttons, appears on the computer screen is not necessarily "real."

Much of this involves questions of "sources" about which I wrote some things earlier. Here again the very topics chosen by some historians enter. One problem with social or gender or religious or sexual history is the paucity and the fragmentary nature of materials with which they must patch their narratives together and form their conclusions. When the subjects are more recent political or international history, the problem is the opposite: a multiplicity of materials on so many different levels of societies and of governments. The records of telephone talks, teletypes, e-mail, etc., may or may not be retrievable; but, even if so, how reliable (or complete) are they? Or: where and what kinds of records of clandestine agencies such as the CIA are retrievable (or indeed reliable) at all? One day the powers of states, as we still know them, will weaken or fade away: but not yet. And, after all, is most of history not the result of the practices and relations of powers? Is it not regrettable, therefore, that the teaching of political and international and military history have now been — and how thoughtlessly — allowed to diminish and in places even disappear?

I write "international history" because, for some time now, we must consider and deal with the complex sources and evidences not only of the relations of states but of those of entire nations and peoples, including their contacts, commerce, sentiments, images of other peoples. These circumstances and conditions include, too, the overall presence of nationalisms in the minds of peoples. How is it — for example — that most American "conservatives" who proclaim their opposition to Big Government favor all kinds of military spending, and support the sending of more and more American troops into the midst of peoples and countries of which they know nothing? Is not nationalism the viscous cement that still holds otherwise less and less cohesive peoples and classes and societies together?

But the ignorance of others — including the ignorance of people and classes of their own nation — is not a monopoly of conservatives. This is a tendency to which historians, too, are not immune. Here is what to me is a trenchant example of American professional historians around 1950. Look at the dates of their — still revered and considered "seminal" — works: Hofstadter, *The American Political Tradition,* 1948; Trilling, *The Liberal Imagination,* 1950; Boorstin, *The Genius of American Politics,* 1953; Potter, *People of Plenty,* 1954; Hartz, *The American Liberal Tradition,* 1955. Consider but the titles of their books. There is one thesis in all of them: that, unlike in Europe or elsewhere, in the United States there is only one intellectual tradition, a perennially liberal one. Now these books, with their general ideas and theses sweeping across the history of the American mental and political and intellectual and ideological landscape, appeared at the very time, 1948–55, when in the United States a popular antiliberal movement arose that began to name itself as "conservative." In 1953 polls reported that about one-half of the American people supported the ideas of Joseph McCarthy. In 1956 the Republican Party's platform called for the establishment of American naval and air bases, "strategically dispersed at home and around the world." By 1960 President Eisenhower himself called himself on occasion "a conservative." In 1964 the Republican Party's presidential candidate Goldwater proclaimed that he was a conservative. In 1980 the declared conservative Ronald Reagan was elected president by an overwhelming majority. By that time more Americans chose to identify themselves as conservatives than as liberals. For many people "liberal" had become a word to be avoided. This was a tectonic development, the origins and the beginnings of which the above-mentioned leading American historians were twenty-five or thirty years before unable to recognize.

We — and they — have had another, though related, problem, which is the difference between ideas and beliefs. They may overlap, indeed they often overlap: but they are not the same things. Throughout my life, as also in this little book, I have insisted on the tremendous importance of ideas for historians. But ideas cannot be separated from the men and women who choose and adopt and express and represent them. How do they invade conscious thinking? Difficult problems, these, which are compounded with the overlapping of ideas and beliefs and faiths. This has been almost always thus, whence there is not much sense to attempt their philosophic or linguistic definitions. But there may be another, perhaps more recent difficulty: a difference between what people think they believe and what they really believe. This differs both from religious beliefs that people had professed earlier, and also from the, now also older, vice of hypocrisy — that is, the difference between what people think and what they actually say or do. A detection and presentation of such questions of belief may be beyond even the tasks of superb historians. Great seers and writers may yet arise to describe them. Around 1950 two sensitive American Catholic writers attempted such: Flannery O'Connor and J. F. Powers, who somehow understood that hypocrisy, the preoccupation of great novelists in the nineteenth century, had been a frequent habit then, but one that now belongs to a past . . .

Yes, there was a time when people were much concerned with what other people believed. The Inquisition in Spain was preoccupied with the "conversos," Jews who had professed their conversion to Catholic Christianity: were they sincere or not? Yet even the auditors and the inquisitors were largely dependent on "intentions gathered from acts" — that is, tangible evidences of whether the conversos were not secretly indulging in their older Jewish practices. Whatever the gathering of the inquisitors' evidences, their problems and purposes aimed to ascertain the sincerity, the genuineness of the accused people's faith. Our problems are different now. We may face new structures of events, because of new structures of ideas: perhaps not so much *what* people think and believe but why? and how? and when? — the last of these three questions having become as important as the other two. Ah! historians' tasks are no longer simple, for many, many reasons, including the condition that people are no longer simple — whether they are educated or not.

SEVEN

Tradition, Inheritance, Imagination

The passing of an entire age ◆ Further development of historical consciousness ◆ Will technology outlast history? ◆ ". . . the hope that from now on a new kind of thinking may begin . . ."

I.

"Historical thinking has now entered our very blood." One result of this is the present recognition, at least for some of us in the West, that an entire historical age has passed, or is passing. This "recognition"—for many, not more than a sense—is often feeble, more than often uneasy: nonetheless it exists. Many people are reluctant to face it—perhaps especially Americans. Historians, too, are often reluctant to state it, since it is such a broad generalization. Yet we ought to recognize the very significance of such a recognition, which is something that did not exist in the past (or at least not in the way it exists for us now). The very term The Middle Ages, its very concept, did not appear until well after its passing. (The designation did not become current until about 1700 and even after.) The term "modern," applied to a succeeding new age, became current afterward. It is still current, even though less and less accurate (or even reasonable). Gibbon thought that it would last for a long time, perhaps forever, because barbarianism was receding just about everywhere, and fast. We, less than three hundred years later, have few grounds for that kind of optimism.

This may be a particular problem, or dilemma, for Americans, whose nation and state and creed were formed in the eighteenth century, in the middle of The Modern Age. I am not American-born (and perhaps an inveterate pessimist), whence perhaps two of my short essay-like books, *The Passing of the Modern Age* (1970) and *The End of the Twentieth Century and the End of the Modern Age* (1993). They were well received by my (few) American readers because (or so I think) they too had begun to recognize that whether an entire historical age was disappearing or not, its very designation of "modern," with its suggestion of something new and everlasting, was (and is) at least open to question.

In these books, but also elsewhere, I wrote that The Modern Age was too imprecise a term, indeed so imprecise as to be unhistorical. On occasion I argued in favor of designating the period of the, say, four hundred years before the mid-twentieth century as The Bourgeois Age, marked as these centuries were by the gradual change from aristocratic to bourgeois rule — but knowing, too, that adjectives may color but because of their very nature precise they are not. Later I came to think that perhaps the entire 1500–1950 period ought to be called The European Age. For many reasons; among them "Europe" replacing the Mediterranean as the main theater of history after about 1500; and then because of the discovery and the possession and colonization and settlement of much of the globe by Europe's powers and by some of their peoples after 1500. However, note that in such a chronological framework "1500" is a generalized and necessarily imprecise date, while "1950" (I could have written "1945") is somewhat more precise, for it was then that The European Age had come to its end, and it was also then that the retreat of European powers from many parts of the world, and also the retreat of the once European settlers, had begun, and probably irreversibly so.

Anyhow: it is arguable and more rather than less evident that by the beginning of the twenty-first century much of an age that began about five centuries ago has passed. And also that the twentieth was an especially transient century (of course every century is transient in some ways), but the twentieth was, historically thinking and speaking, a short century too, seventy-five years long, from 1914 to 1989, marked by two gigantic world wars (and then the so-called Cold War was but a consequence of the Second). No reason here to argue further what is, or should be, obvious. But for the purposes of this little book I am compelled to state something that is related to the foregoing but also less obvious: that our present consciousness of history has been one of the stellar achievements of The European Age.

2.

Existence within history, interest in history, recording of history, writing history, all had elements of consciousness within them: but sometime in the sixteenth and especially seventeenth centuries, mostly in Western Europe and England, a new, wider, and deeper sense of a historical consciousness began to appear. I described some of its features earlier in this book, including its many consequences, of which the practice of professional historianship was but one. Here and there I have gone far enough to suggest that, while the growth of historical consciousness has been of course less widespread than the tremendous and worldwide applications of the scientific method, it *may* have been more deep-going than the latter (and not merely because of professional historianship). In any event, the latter was European and then American and so it remained for a relatively long time. Not until the early twentieth century do we find Asian and Japanese and Chinese historians adopting the professional practices of their European and American colleagues, going thus beyond the unquestioning acceptance and recording of legendary events in their own countries — indications of the widening and, on occasion, deepening sense of history across the world.

It may even be part and parcel of something else: a reversal of Woodrow Wilson's ideological shibboleth "to make the world safe for democracy," still pursued and declared by many American politicians. *To make democracy safe for the world* is, or ought to be, a more modest but also more profound task, dependent on domestic achievements and potential examples, in the recognition and promotion of which teachers and writers of history have their roles to play. And that role — in the honest meaning of a nowadays often wrongly used adjective — is truly *conservative*. The finest historians during the past two hundred years knew and represented and exemplified this. Two of them, Burckhardt and Huizinga, *primi inter pares,* lived in the very midst, in or near the peak of The Bourgeois Age, and in bourgeois circumstances: but they were patricians rather than bourgeois, and very European. They were not dogmatically liberal, nor were they progressives. It may be telling that they came from and taught and wrote in small

Western European countries, Switzerland and Holland. Burckhardt's Greek and Roman and Renaissance histories are renderings of ancient matters, illuminating them for us to see. His *On History and Historians* comprises paragraphs of great insights (originally in lectures to his students). Huizinga's *The Waning of the Middle Ages* gives us a rendering of what and how some people were thinking more than five hundred years ago, when most of those people were not aware what those transformations were: but we are. "Waning" and "Middle Ages" would have made no sense to them: but to us, yes (and in more than one way).

Burckhardt and Huizinga and Tocqueville and many, many fine historians, necessarily unnamed or even unlisted here, creditably attempted to suggest and describe and even prove what and how some people were thinking at a particular time and in a particular place. With this interest in the history of ideas and beliefs they were forerunners of the recent historians of "mentalités." And their examples have not been in vain. To give one recent example: in the admittedly complicated and difficult sphere of church and religious history, English and Irish historians have attempted to penetrate, collect, assemble, and interpret fragments of evidences of changes of behavior and belief within the confused and confusing conditions of sixteenth-century England. These contemporary professional colleagues of ours exemplify the widening and deepening approaches and perceptions of history attempted by their above-mentioned great predecessors. Only: how much of these endeavors will endure?

3.

We have already entered an age where the influence (and consequently the importance) of books has been decreasing. So has that of the printed word.* There is no reason to believe that this devolution will be reversed soon, or at all. But history, as *we* know it, is hardly separable from the written word. What will happen to history when books will disappear?

History, as I have argued, is (and was, and will be) more than the recorded past; but the remembered past,

* One recent example, affecting me. The handbook of instructions accompanying the computer I recently bought contains almost one hundred pages. It does *not* include a single printed instruction of how to use this machine for writing. Nor does it include anything about its keyboard, which, in addition to keys for letters and numbers, has more than thirty other keys, buttons, figures, icons. At the bottom of the computer screen there are two dozen pictorial icons, among them only one that enables me to use the computer for writing. The helpful personnel of the computer store to which I must repair to gather further instructions tell me that among the hundreds of people crowding into the store at almost any hour of the working day I may be one of the very few, indeed perhaps the only one, who uses the computer mainly for writing. (The others come there to learn or improve their use of it for pictures, music, games, etc.)

too, is variable and imperfect, smaller as it is than the entire past. A sense of the past — some kind of interest in it, and even a kind of respect for a knowledge of it — will always exist. But with what results? Is it possible that interest in "the past" may altogether absorb "history" (including the professional study of the latter)? Storytelling (and story watching) will not disappear; but history writing may.

I doubt that centuries from now books will entirely disappear — I am inclined to think that book readers will still exist, though a very small minority. Collectors of books (of all kinds, and for all kinds of reasons) will also exist, I hope more of them than the still existing collectors of parchments and scrolls. We do not know. I do not know. Four or five centuries ago the emergence of a historical consciousness was an achievement of The European Age. So was the method of modern science and its applications. Which of the two will endure longer? Will a further development of historical consciousness have an effect on the applications of mechanical science? Will technology dominate history more and more — or less and less? (*Not* impossible, that.) But meanwhile machines and their applications have already affected the practices of the study and writing of history that we know. Already there are many thousands of historical articles and results of researches that are available for those interested in them but *not* in print. That this will go on and on — who can doubt that? That they will (and it has already begun to) affect the thinking of people, not only *what* they think but *how* they think, is evident too. There will be changes in the very consciousness of people: but how, or what, I cannot know.

What I know is the acuity of some of Tocqueville's insights written more than 170 years ago, in the second volume of his *Democracy in America*. He saw that "the habit of inattention" is "the greatest defect of democratic character." A throwaway sentence but a very profound one — and of something that even he could not foresee, the mutation from a verbal to a pictorial age. In the same book he wrote something that, sadly, professional historians ought to think about, concerning the present and the future of their subject and craft:

> Because the civilization of ancient Rome perished in consequence of the invasion of Barbarians, we are perhaps apt to think that civilization cannot perish in any other manner. If the light by which we are guided is ever extinguished, it will dwindle by degrees and expire of itself. By dint of close adherence to mere applications, principles would be lost sight of; and when the principles were wholly forgotten, the methods derived from them would be ill pursued.

New methods would no longer be invented, and men would continue, without intelligence and art, to apply scientific processes no longer understood.

Professional historiography, professional historianship, may one day disappear. But of one condition of human consciousness I remain certain. This is men's interest in and respect for the past. I can also believe that centuries from now people will have a respect for the five hundred years of The European Age, comparable to what the sudden blossoming respect men of the Renaissance had for the achievements of Greece and Rome. Comparable: but not identical. That admiration, six or more centuries ago, was often uncritical, and therefore unhistorical. It included, among other things, the rejection of many things in the Middle Ages, many of its achievements. Such a rejection of an entire epoch passing now will not happen. There will be no hearkening back to an idealized epoch that had preceded the last one. Our historical consciousness is more advanced than that.

In George Orwell's dystopian novel *Nineteen Eighty-Four,* written shortly before the middle of the twentieth century — an important book, but not one of Orwell's best — he presaged a brutal political and tyrannical world, where science and its applications had been abandoned and stopped (well: the very opposite has happened); *but* where "Winston Smith" (born in 1945: his first name is significant) on one occasion raises his glass and says a toast to The Past. I, for one, do not think that this respect — and love — for the past is bound to disappear.

4.

History is unpredictable. More precisely: more than often history is wrongly predicted by people who project (or, rather, imagine) the progress of things and tendencies that to them seem to flourish at the present. Instead, coming close to ending this little book, a large question: is the triumph of "science" over "history" inevitable? It is not. Consider that science is a portion of history but not the reverse: first came nature, then came man, and then the science of nature. No scientists, no science — though applications of science will remain. No historians, no history? Well, not only much of the past but much of the knowledge of the past will remain.

Let me repeat Wendell Berry's chilling but truly prophetic thought: that the future may be divided between men who think of themselves as machines, and men who think of themselves as creatures. This is very possible and plausible; I see this division already happening (whether political or social thinkers or actors are aware of this or not). I fear that people who think of themselves as God's creatures may be a minority (at least for a while). And, within that minority, how many different ways of beliefs may exist, or sprout? But, more important: is it certain, is it irretrievable that men (and, perhaps, especially women) will be long content with thinking of themselves as machines? We have now passed from a humanistic to a mechanistic age. That, too, will not last forever.

Consider a condition, unthought and ignored now. This is that even our most complex, incredible, and at times even unimaginable machines function entirely dependent on mechanical causality — which is but one form of causality, and the limitations of which have already been demonstrated in subatomic physics, that is, in the very study of matter. And while mechanical causality is of course insufficient to explain human nature, so a time may come when its limitations may affect and even transform the applications of "natural science."

Enough of this. Our concern is with history, which is the knowledge of human beings, past or present, of other human beings. Reminding people of these innumerable and endless (and also mysterious) connections of the present and the past is a principal task of historians, perhaps especially in our times. They must see themselves as more than specialists of a traditional form of knowledge. They ought to see themselves as humble but steadfast guardians of civilization — protecting, practicing, cultivating, preserving its verbal and written tradition, during the coming of a pictorial and primitive and increasingly abstract age: votaries of the written word, prophets not of a future but of an ever increasing past. Thus they must regard themselves, and thus should they be regarded by others. A large responsibility, this, and little cause for contentment. Historians are not better or worse than are other human beings, wherefore their self-satisfaction with the recognition of their professional historianship is needlessly shallow. Among other important matters they ought to know that the equality of people, and of men and women, does not and should not mean uniformity but the recognition and protection of the potentiality of every human being.

Still: good, even remarkably good, history is being taught and written and published even now. There are small historical journals, with limited circulations, struggling on and on: the standards of their reviews (of course dependent on their editors' choices of the reviewers) are still often good. This corresponds to the circumstance, especially in the United States after about 1970, that many of the best professional teachers and writers of history may now be found in the nooks and crannies of little-known institutions of higher education, across this vast country. Few of these, so often lonely, paragons of a once so reputable and honorable profession are categorical conservatives or dogmatic liberals. Many of them are women who had chosen to enter the ranks of professional historians not so long ago.

They must recognize that human nature does not accord with the "laws" of physics — that, for example, while it is easier to wrestle with a weak man than with a strong one, it is more difficult to wrestle with a weak mind than with a strong one. Or: while it is more and more difficult to force more and more stuff into a box or bag or bottle already filled, it is easier to add more and more knowledge to the amount we already know. Or: "intolerable" is what — and when — people think they ought no longer tolerate. Etc., etc. In sum: what matters is what and how and when people think. In sum: professional historians, perhaps even more than others, must recognize (or at least be well aware) that the condition, indeed the very nature, of historical knowledge is not "scientific" knowledge, not mechanically causal, and not determined. And so it must be taught, and written — and, of course, thought.

About the future: Werner Heisenberg in a lecture but a few weeks before he died, in 1976: ". . . the hope that from now on a new kind of thinking may begin, something that in our time may be sensed rather than described yet."*

* "Die Hoffnung, dass von hier eine neue, weitere Art des Denkens ihre Ausgang nehmen koennte, die in unserer Zeit allerdings eher geahnt als beschrieben werden kann." *Gesammette Werke* (Munich, 1985), 3:540.

Here and there I have tried.

Apologia

Through a now very long lifetime of historianship and writing I chose, more than often, not to add Introductions or Conclusions to my books — their contents ought to speak for themselves. But for the sake of this book I feel compelled to add an Apologia (which Introductions and Conclusions often implicitly are, whether their authors know that or not).

Mine has been an unusual career, and in more than one way. Its dualities are relevant to this book. I was a teacher, a professor of history in a small college, and only occasionally in large universities, during almost fifty years. But I was also a writer of history at the same time, producing about twenty books during my teaching years, and more after that. Books about different subjects, at times ignored by specialists in their subjects, wrongly so, even though the standards of my researches and the qualities of my historical narratives were sufficient, to say the least.

But I understand — and "comprendre c'est pardonner" — my critics' unease. A "prolific" writer — an adjective that I myself do not like at all. And a historian whose many books have been published by "trade" publishers, and most of them written not primarily for academics but, at their best, straddling the fence between professional historianship and history written for many kinds of readers interested in their subjects.

For this I will not offer, or even think about, an apology. I have said in this book what I said numberless times before: that history does not have a language of its own, that it should be, and it is, not only written but taught and spoken and thought for almost anyone capable of reading. This conviction of mine is deeper and stronger than the commercial and financial advantages (there have been few) that accrue from the sale of some of my books to "the general public" here and abroad. Yet I understand, too, how to many of my former and current professional colleagues a "straddler" may also suggest "marginal" (or to some of them even "arrogant" or "daring"). Against the epithet of arrogance let me say that I have long known the limits of my learning. (I *am* a traditionalist about many things — but, for instance, I know little Greek, though some Latin.) And when it comes to historical philosophy or epistemology of which this book is about, I take at least some comfort from the condition that at the present state of a decaying civilization a few statements of common sense may give the impression that their author is a profound thinker.

This brings me to the other duality — or ambivalence; or ambiguity; or "straddling" — of my publications, indeed of myself. Throughout my working life I have had two quite different, though parallel, and often overlapping interests. One of them was (and perhaps still is) to write historical descriptions of exceptional quality. The other (look at this book) is my ceaseless questioning of what historical knowledge really *is* — eventually suggesting a historical philosophy that is the obverse of a philosophy of history. "Ceaseless," because these two preoccupations lived together, they existed in my mind at the same time. For example: I worked on my book *Historical Consciousness,* drafting and rewriting it during thirteen years, 1955 until its publication in 1968, while I wrote and published three other smaller books. (*Historical Consciousness* then had two other editions, 1985 and 1994; to them I added substantial chapters, because my interest in its subjects had widened and grown.) And then I returned to its subjects again and again, in articles and essays and reviews and public lectures. And in portions of other books of mine, for instance at the end of *The End of the Twentieth Century and the End of the Modern Age,* 1993; throughout in the very different *At the End of the Modern Age,* 2002; in the very first portion ("A Bad Fifteen Minutes") of a kind of late autobiography, *Last Rites,* 2009; and now, in the eighty-seventh year of my life, writing an entire book, this one, about the present and the future of history to be published in 2011.

But why? Ah! there are so many things that compel a man to write a book about this or that. Yet one — though *not* the most important — element in this instance is that these works of mine that I consider may be, or even are, my most important achievements, have been largely — and very largely — unknown. There is a melancholy coincidence here. After about 1970, when the chaotic crisis of Western civilization and culture had come to affect the profession of historianship, a cottage industry came into being, attempting to deal with what history "is" — writers and periodicals, such as *History and Theory,* whose editors chose to make no mention of my above-listed works, to the extent of excluding the titles even from the very extensive lists of their bibliographies. I, on the other side of the fence (if "fence" it is), find these relatively recent books and articles about the philosophy of history, etc., largely substanceless and often unreadable. Never mind! Their very existence at least suggests that some of these scholars and philosophizers are beginning to be interested in some of the questions and problems that have plagued me for so many years. I am as vain as any man: but vain rather than jealous: throughout my career I was relieved when I found that somebody else has written a book that I had thought should be written.

Oh! Good, serious historians, dedicated to their teaching and writing: please just skim over my many *obiter dicta* in this little book, and forgive my occasional sarcastic sayings about the profession. I greet you, I lift my hat to honor your work, your very existence. I am bald and white-haired, but the lifting my hat matters. I think that is more than a gesture: it is a fact. (All right: a feat. See page 83.)